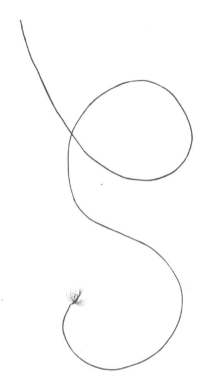

Simple Fly Fishing

Techniques for Tenkara and Rod & Reel
Yvon Chouinard, Craig Mathews, and Mauro Mazzo

REVISED SECOND EDITION

Foreword by Russell Chatham, Paintings by James Prosek

patagonia®

Simple Fly Fishing
Techniques for Tenkara and Rod & Reel

Patagonia publishes a select list of titles on wilderness, wildlife, and outdoor sports that inspire and restore a connection to the natural world.

Revised Edition
Printed in Canada on 100 percent post-consumer recycled paper.

Editor – John Dutton
Book Designer – Christina Speed
Illustrator – Erik Brooks
Project Manager – Jennifer Patrick
Photo Editors – Jane Sievert, Jennifer Ridgeway
Graphic Production – Emma Wilson, Rafael Dunn

Creative Director – Bill Boland
Creative Advisor – Jennifer Ridgeway
Director of Books – Karla Olson

Paperback ISBN 978-1-938340-79-6
E-Book ISBN 978-1-938340-80-2
Library of Congress Control Number 2013957437

ENVIRONMENTAL BENEFITS STATEMENT
Patagonia Inc saved the following resources by printing the pages of this book on chlorine free paper made with 100% post-consumer waste.

TREES	WATER	ENERGY	SOLID WASTE	GREENHOUSE GASES
139 FULLY GROWN	11,000 GALLONS	59 MILLION BTUs	480 POUNDS	59,900 POUNDS

Environmental impact estimates were made using the Environmental Paper Network Paper Calculator 40. For more information visit www.papercalculator.org.

Publisher's Cataloging in Publication Data
Chouinard, Yvon, 1938-

Simple fly fishing : techniques for tenkara and rod & reel / Yvon Chouinard, Craig Mathews, and Mauro Mazzo. -- Ventura, Calif. : Patagonia Books, 2014.

p. ; cm.

ISBN: 978-1-938340-27-7 ; 978-1-938340-28-4 (ebook)
Includes bibliography.
Summary: The best way to catch trout is simply, with a rod and a fly and not much else. Discover where the fish are, at what depth, and what they are feeding on. This book describes the techniques needed to present a fly, make it look lifelike, and hook the fish. Chapters on wet flies, nymphs, and dry flies, the authors employ both the tenkara rod as well as regular fly fishing gear. Paintings by renowned artist James Prosek, technical illustrations, and inspiring photographs and stories throughout.--Publisher.

1. Fly fishing--Handbooks, manuals, etc. 2. Tenkara fly fishing--Handbooks, manuals, etc. 3. Trout fishing--Handbooks, manuals, etc. 4. Fishing tackle. 5. Fishing rods. 6. Fishing lures. I. Mathews, Craig. II. Mazzo, Mauro. III. Title.

SH456 .C56 2014   2013957437
799.12/4--dc23   1404

Contents

Dusk on the Blackfoot River. Russell Chatham

FOREWORD
Russell Chatham

The fact is that fishing with an artificial fly has always been an elitist activity. Simply stated, the reason is that at its core lies a set of esthetic precepts rather fundamentally at odds with those of the common man whose approach to life's various aspects is simple practicality. Be that as it may, at the end of the day fishing is still just fishing.

Going back to its origins in Europe, fly casting was practiced in the realm of the aristocracy who owned and controlled the trout and salmon waters appropriate to its use. However, in the literature there sometimes would appear poachers who fell in love with the esoteric essence of this enterprise, and who were willing to risk imprisonment for the sake of its sensual rewards.

Once transposed to America it became a tad more democratic; but just a tad, as wealthy easterners commandeered private waters in the Catskills and Adirondacks and formed exclusive clubs in New York.

Enter the left coast, where many regarded the right as some version of an anthropomorphic museum filled with taxidermied throwbacks, and where fly fishing was mainstream from the start among the great unwashed. In spite of this, it has degenerated into a country club activity popular with the nouveau riche in which the accoutrements have become so ridiculously complex and expensive that Joe Six-Pack can only stand helplessly with his nose pressed to the tackle store window.

One has to wonder how this happened. There are several very simple explanations. The first and most important is that because of our universal environmental crimes, we've ruined most of the fishing close to home: the all-important free fishing that youngsters could readily find after school on foot or by bike.

Because of this, in the late 1970s companies like Fishing International and Frontiers began booking exotic world travel directed at, but not exclusive to, fly fishermen. This changed the angling pastime precipitously. Now, instead of throwing your waders and rod into the trunk of the car and driving for an hour from San Francisco to the Russian River, you wrote a check for a thousand dollars a day to go to Alaska, British Columbia, South America, Iceland, or Russia.

> The more complex technology is allowed to intrude upon the fundamental simplicity of fishing, the further one becomes removed from its core value.
>
> *– Russell Chatham*

It didn't take the tackle companies long to go on a high-alert point. Suddenly, rods didn't cost twenty-five dollars anymore. Now, instead of plebeian fiberglass, they were made of graphite or boron technology and could set you back four, five, or even six hundred dollars. And the gold- and silver-plated reels that had all the class of a three-dollar whore's earrings were similarly priced. Alright Bucko, if you can afford eight or nine thousand dollars to wet a line for a week, you need the Right Stuff.

It's simple, greed-driven supply-side undemocratic capitalism doing what it does best, which is to demand more and more product and ever-increasing sales. Product lifespan is earmarked at the factory for the flea market, and the manufacturers will handle the public relations on that.

As the great rod designer and builder Tom Morgan has said over and over again, "A good rod is a good rod whether it was made sixty years or sixty days ago." And in this he was echoing the sentiments of every knowledgeable and ethical fine craftsman. But that's not how you sell more rods. First, yesterday's must be categorized as inferior and obsolete. In its place you need some new chemical component with a technical-sounding name and a guarantee to make you a better caster. I remember once about thirty years ago being in Dan Bailey's Fly Shop in Livingston, Montana, when a tourist was considering buying a four-hundred-dollar fly rod. The sales associate at the time, Fred Terwilliger, suggested they go out on the train depot lawn across the street and cast it. Pretty soon they were back in the store and Fred said, "Mister, you don't need a four-hundred-dollar rod, you need a fifty-dollar casting lesson."

With respect to fly lines, with the exception of a perfectly level one, which is useless, there are only three basic designs. The most traditional of these is the double taper. Historically, the reason for this was that when all lines were made of silk, you fished half the day with one end, and when it began to sink, you turned it around, greased up the new end, and went back to fishing. The weight-forward taper has a heavier section toward the front, designed to fish at greater distances. You false cast this belly, as it's called, then shoot it, pulling the thinner fly line out behind it. A shooting taper, or head, is generally thirty feet long, tied to monofilament, making it the ultimate tool for distance casting. The first two styles, often referred to as whole lines, are generally about ninety to a hundred feet in length. All of these either float, or else sink at varying speeds.

I recall quite clearly in the 1950s when Scientific Anglers introduced the first plastic lines (heretofore, fly lines were woven of silk, nylon, or Dacron fibers). They produced the three aforementioned styles in white, which floated, and dark green, which sank. They

Westslope cutthroat and bull trout.
Flathead River, Montana. *Patrick Clayton*

worked closely with, and listened to, onetime world-record caster My-ron Gregory, who brought to the table all the physical knowledge of the R.L. Winston Rod Company ("Rod Builder to the Champions") and the Golden Gate Angling and Casting Club, both in San Francisco.

A year or so ago, I went through a new Scientific Anglers cata-logue. In it were pictured and described about eighty different fly lines. Eighty. It seems that a line good for Florida's west coast is all wrong for its east coast, and of course neither are suitable for the Keys. And the line that's correct for Chesapeake Bay will not do for the Jersey Shore, and of course is also dead wrong for the flats around Nantucket. And don't get the idea that you can transpose your British Columbia steelhead line to Iceland's Atlantic salmon rivers. How naïve can you get? And so on until the minutiae becomes a spinning top whirling to the kachinging of the cash register.

The all-time perfect system in distance casting for steelhead and salmon as well as tournament events was developed in San Francisco in the 1940s and perfected in the 1950s. It was simply a thirty-foot shooting head for fishing, and fifty for competition, backed by ny-lon monofilament. Early on, this material was very hard to handle, being wiry and easily tangled. Eventually however, the Sunset Line and Twine Company in Petaluma, California, developed a brand they

Russell Chatham in old-school coveralls and old-school wooden boat, Paradise Valley, Montana. *Russell Chatham Collection*

called Amnesia that eliminated those problems.

What disturbed the fly line manufacturers to the point of distraction was that this running line cost the user about a nickel a mile, so it was systematically denigrated in ads and articles. Soon, an array of more costly substitutes began coming on the market, not one of which ever came close to achieving the perfect efficiency of Amnesia. What this did was cause people to buy thousands of yards of expensive ineffective shooting line, thereby completely destroying the shooting head's real value.

Because of this the stage was set for something new, or rather something old retooled and pressed back into service. It's been some twenty years now, I suppose, since the appearance of the two-handed rod fad. The glamour fish are the sea trout and salmon, and as a general rule, catching them requires a longish cast. To become genuinely proficient at distance casting with a traditional one-handed nine-foot fly rod requires 10,000 hours of practice, and people who can afford to pay eight to fifteen thousand dollars a week to go fishing don't have that kind of time to practice because they're too busy making money.

I learned about double-handed casting from some Scottish gentlemen who visited San Francisco in the 1950s. The rather autoerotic version(s) of Spey casting as now practiced in America would be unrecognizable to these men. I've been everywhere on the planet where you can fish for anadromous fish, and have watched with mild amusement as the captains of industry strained, slashed, and grunted out fishable casts, only to just stand there like designated rod holders devoted to supporting their enormous tackle while the huge lines swung with the current, the owners unable to manipulate the fly—the central act in fishing.

I've seen many times and in many places men and women learning to make fishable casts in a short day. A little whooshing, a little swishing, and with a flourish the fly, probably an absurdly large one, plops down at eighty feet every time. Perfect. Now the good news for the industry: technology that puts anglers in the bucket comes with a curse involving their checkbooks. Forget six hundred for the advantage of a very long rod; now it's a thousand. And you'll also need a bigger, much more expensive and uglier reel, not to mention a large bag full of specialized fly lines.

Many people, myself included, first learned to fish with a stick of some kind, probably willow, with a piece of line attached to it at the end of which was a hook and a wiggly worm. This ultimately low-tech accessory put the young angler in the closest proximity to the water and the quarry. Wet shoes and pant legs were ubiquitous. Here was the essential undergraduate course that instilled an intimate love of fishing so that no matter what brand of sophistication followed throughout the years, those early memories were etched forever.

So it is: the more complex technology is allowed to intrude upon the fundamental simplicity of fishing, the further one becomes removed from its core value. At its most profound, fishing is a way of remaining forever a child. Of course, we cannot truly do that, nor should we want to, but the illusion of it is one important key to mental health.

All concerned people in this country wish that the upcoming generation would spend more time out in the natural world. There are some conservationists who are opposed to fishing and hunting, but I'm sorry, they are not thinking it through. In order to transpose mere interest into passionate love requires proactive behavior. The road is an uphill one because today's youth of the digital world are raised with offers of passive, instant gratification. Can a person raised in that environment ever fish all day without a bite? Maybe it should be mandatory for schools to provide environmental study from grade one in which there is no computer involved, or any other electronic visual aid, only calm, analytical conversation mixed in with visits to if not wild places at least rural ones.

This brings us around to the tenkara style, a perfect way to eliminate mechanical moving parts, an homage as it were to the willow branch. I'm not a trout fisherman, so my long Japanese rod is used on still waters near where I live in Northern California.

In the fading light of a perfectly quiet evening last November, I was standing by a beautiful pond. To my left, a pair of mallards noodled around the lily pads and red-winged blackbirds trilled their beautiful song, while a bullfrog announced his presence from the tules on my right. My pant legs and shoes were wet and muddy, and as the sun dipped behind the hills I started to shiver. I danced a little fly across the water and six-inch bluegills raced to hit it. Time stood still. I was an eleven-year-old boy again, sneaking concealed along Sleepy Hollow Creek, advancing toward a bay tree root where I knew there were baby steelhead hiding. Mom said not to be late for dinner, but I wasn't hungry. I was as happy as you can get.

An angler with a "loop rod." Artwork for the first fishing book published (in 1496) in English: *A Treatyse of Fysshynge Wyth an Angle*, by Dame Juliana Berners.

INTRODUCTION
Yvon Chouinard

Why write one more book about fishing when there are probably more books on the subject than romance novels?

Since the fifteenth century, every nuance of fly fishing has been written about in the utmost detail, leaving us to endlessly reinvent what has already been discovered. A tiny change on a classic fly and the "inventor" gets to name it after himself and collect a dime for each one sold. Many of the books on technique are like business books where a minor theory is spread out over three hundred pages, when all it really merits is a magazine article.

Heaven knows we fly fishers are suckers for every new gizmo we think will give us a leg up on catching fish. We wear vests with twenty pockets and waders with even more storage. And as if that isn't enough, we have lanyards, waist packs, and backpacks to carry even more impedimenta. Hundreds of fly lines are now available to us, yet I seriously doubt you will catch one more trout with a line fine-tuned to the conditions than with a classic double taper. The no-nonsense fly fisher Rob Brown, from Terrace, British Columbia, looking over a steelheader's array of fly boxes filled with hundreds of garish flies, said it best when he asked, "When did the green-butt stop working for you?"

I would offer that this proliferation of gear is supported by busy people who lack for nothing in their lives except time. Our "time-saving" communication devices, like tablets and smartphones, make slaves of their owners. We are unwilling, or unable, to put in the 10,000 hours needed to become a master fisher, hunter, or mountain climber. Instead, we load up with all the latest stuff and hire guides to do everything for us—including tying on the fly and releasing the fish. The guides have become enablers rather than teachers. How many bonefish would average anglers catch if they had to work out the tides and wade and spot fish themselves instead of waiting for a guide to bark, "Ten o'clock, forty-foot cast now! Wait . . . strip . . . strip"? The guides leave clients so unsure of themselves that they think there must be some secret, unattainable knowledge that only the guide possesses.

Despite rumors to the contrary, the paramount objective is: to catch fish…

– Sheridan Anderson, The Curtis Creek Manifesto

As author Sheridan Anderson says in *The Curtis Creek Manifesto*, the objective of fishing is to catch fish, but in the pursuit of the catch you will gain so much more. The higher purpose of practicing a sport such as fly fishing, hunting, or mountain climbing is to affect a spiritual and physical gain. But if the process is compromised, there is no transformation.

Fishing with a fly can be such an incredibly complex and passionate sport that no one can fully master all the different disciplines in one lifetime. Some anglers prefer to limit themselves to only fishing with dry flies, while others specialize in perfecting their casting, fly tying, or even learning the Latin names and life history of all the insects. These can be legitimate endeavors in themselves, and there are untold books written about these subjects. This book is not one of them.

This is a book for the young person who wants to learn but feels intimidated by the complexity, elitism, and expense of the sport. He sees his father who owns multiple thousand-dollar rods and reels, fishes only with guides at five hundred-plus dollars a day (plus mandatory tips), and flies all over the world to stay at luxury lodges. And the son thinks, "This is not for me."

It is also for the woman and her daughter who are put off by the image of the testosterone-fueled "rip-some-lips," good-old-boy, bass and trout fisherman who has turned the "contemplative pastime" into a competitive combat sport.

This is also a book for the experienced angler who has all the gadgets and gizmos and discovers he or she wants to replace all that stuff with skill, knowledge, and simplicity. It is for the person who believes that a design or a piece of art or a sporting endeavor is finalized and mastered "not when there is nothing more to add, but when there is nothing more to take away," as Antoine de Saint-Exupéry advocated.

It's for the person who thinks maybe it's time to look at the raked Zen sand garden with its three stones and see if he or she can convey the same powerful, evocative image of space and balance with only two rocks or even one.

Most anglers soon discover simple fly fishing helps preserve our capacity for wonder. It can teach us to see, smell, and feel the miracles of stream life—with the beauty of nature and serenity all around—as we pursue wild fish.

THE TENKARA ROD

Many of us of a certain age remember our first fishing pole. We would go to the local sporting goods store and buy a long bamboo pole—what was then called a Calcutta. A line, with a worm or fly on the end, was attached to the tip. For centuries, perhaps even before the

Roman mosaic from the Villa of the Nile at Leptis Magna, Jamahiriya Museum, Libya. *Robert Harding, Alamy*

time of Christ, this is the way people all over the world learned to fish—and still do.

Thirty years ago, a Japanese friend gave me a telescoping fiberglass rod with no reel seat. It was a beautiful, precious gift; light, sensitive, and elegant. When I received this rod, I didn't really understand what I was getting, and I stored it on a shelf in my cabin for fifteen years. I have since learned that it is called a tenkara rod, which means "from the heavens," and is used in Japan to fish for yamame, amago, and iwana trout in small mountain streams.

Some years later, I fished the Sesia River in Italy with Mauro Mazzo. He mentioned that the traditional way to fish the Sesia is to use an eleven- to sixteen-foot-long rod with no reel and just a horsehair line tied to the tip. The lines, which are about one or one and a half times the length of the rod, are twisted from the tail of a white stallion, starting with fourteen or sixteen hairs and tapering down to three at the tippet end. A short, nylon tippet is added and one to five soft-hackle flies are tied onto the tippet one foot apart. Casting is done using various overhead, roll, and Spey casts. It's particularly effective in winter with a size 22 purple-body soft hackle for wary and selective grayling. The hackles, made from the very soft feathers of a bird called ciuffolotto, maintain their lifelike action in the river. There are still about twenty practitioners of this technique in Italy, of which ten make their own lines.

The next summer, Mauro and I decided to try the tenkara rod on a willow-lined meadow creek in the Wyoming Range. It was a very

Modern-day Balinese fisherman on the southeast coast of Sanur. *Willem Sorm*

windy day in August, and grasshoppers were being blown about, so we put on a muddler and fished it upstream as a hopper and downstream as a sculpin. The thin, heavy horsehair line cut through the wind far better than a floating fly line. Every bend of the creek had a pool, and we moved from pool to pool without having to reel in line and let it out again. We caught fish in every pool: nice cutthroats up to sixteen inches.

Mauro's girlfriend, Daniela, who had never fished a day in her life, picked up the rod and in less than five minutes landed the biggest cutthroat of the day. "Easy," she said. "What's the big deal?"

I think this centuries-old technique was perfect for fly fishing that day and more effective than anything that has come out of our high-tech fly fishing industry. In fact, this is the same gear and technique traditionally used by French and Japanese market fishers. When your living depends on supplying restaurants and hotels with trout, you're not going to waste money on seven-hundred-dollar rods, five-hundred-dollar reels, and three-dollar flies.

Learning to fish with a tenkara rod and a short line is the easiest way to learn to fly-fish. It can be taught to an eight-year-old in minutes. Put her on a riffle with an old-fashioned soft-hackle fly, and she can outfish dad on the first day. Catching fish right from the start is the way to catch an angler for life. And dad can become a better fisher by applying the lessons learned from this ultimately simple method to fishing with his regular gear.

Kerry Beasley getting one last fish in before the storm moved over Guitar Lake, Sierra Nevada, California. *Austin Trigg*

Other than learning to fish where the fish are, the most important thing an angler can do to catch fish is to control the action of the fly. It's more important than the color or size of the fly, the time of day, or getting off a perfect cast. Why is a worm so effective? Because it is always moving. Why have soft baits replaced hard spoons and lures? Because they bend and flex in enticing ways.

Too many fly fishers are so fixated on launching long casts that they end up putting the fly beyond where the fish are. And with those long casts, they cannot control what the fly is doing.

This is especially true of steelheaders and their long Spey rods: most steelhead are close to the bank, not in the middle of the river. I once watched the great steelheader Harry Lemire fish behind a friend of mine. Lemire was walking the bank, making short casts with a floating line and making his signature fly, the Steelhead Caddis, wake, swim, twitch, and flit around on the surface. He was hooking fish just behind my friend, who was wading deep, casting long, and not catching anything. Control is everything.

In this book, we use the simplest of all fly fishing methods, a pole with a line on the end, to illustrate how to control the fly without the complexity of modern equipment getting in the way. Getting the fly to the depth where the fish are feeding and imparting motion to the fly is critical. This is where the tenkara excels. You will catch fish using simple methods and knowledge, in an elegant and artful way. This is fly fishing at its most basic, and like kayaking without a paddle, it brings you closer to the simple truths of the sport. When you pick up (or go back to) a rod and reel, you will be a more complete angler. I believe you will also enjoy your time on the water more and, to Mr. Anderson's point, catch more fish.

Arturo Pugno
Mauro Mazzo

Every time I sit in front of this "young" guy with those bright eyes that have seen more than eighty springs, I know I am going to learn something. If there is a person who represents the concept of simple fly fishing, it is Arturo.

He has fished for most of his life with the Valsesiana style—a rod with a fixed line (they have been fishing this way for more than 500 years). He started fishing in Italy in the 1940s during the Second World War—the bag limit was twenty fish.

At that time people went fishing for food; catch and release was not an option. Even now, Arturo does not totally understand catch and release. When I am with him, I justify it by the fact that I don't like to eat trout or grayling.

His first fishing teacher was a schoolteacher who took him fishing on Sundays, and from the

Arturo Pugno describes the characteristics of a feather he uses in his wet flies.
Mauro Mazzo

outset Arturo caught more fish than him. He didn't let on though, afraid he was going to hurt his teacher's feelings.

Arturo started to fish on Saturdays as well, but fishing on Saturdays was a risky business. Every Saturday the students were "invited" to do gymnastic exercises—in accordance with the fascist myth of creating a superior race. Arturo had no interest in becoming part of a superior race, he was actually quite skinny—the only thing he wanted to do was fish as often as possible.

An additional problem was that the gymnasium, where the young fascists were training, was very close to the trail he walked to the river. He had to go the long way around to get to the river, but it turns out it was worth the risk. The only thing he still regrets is that he couldn't fish the pool by the gymnasium—that was one of the best on the river.

Arturo didn't pass the final exams for three subjects one year. His mother was surprised, because Arturo was often in his room studying, and he always had schoolbooks on his bedside table. While his mother was in his room one day cleaning up she chanced to open one of his schoolbooks. Right there, between the pages, was a horsehair line under construction. That was the end of the game for Arturo, and he was sent to Turin to learn what discipline means from an uncle who was an army officer.

Luckily after a few months, the uncle was given a different assignment, and Arturo went home to his beloved Sesia—this time determined to steal some time from fishing to complete his studies. He admits that he has never been a good student, though he did manage to finish school and became a teacher himself.

At that time, the teachers worked only in the morning, so he had all afternoon free to go fishing—it was his perfect job. His first assignment was in the village of Erbareti—now completely abandoned—with no electricity or water. He slept in the school and the main night life attraction was to recite the rosary

with the old local women. After the first night of doing that, he decided he would explore every inch of the local stream instead.

He worked one year in Erbareti, then moved to another mountain village, a little bigger, on the Mastallone River—this made life more pleasant. Finally, he was assigned to a school in Varallo, on the river where he spent most of his fishing life: his beloved Sesia.

When he started fishing during the Second World War, the biggest problem was finding good hooks. Most of the steel industry production was destined for other things—as you can imagine.

He liked to tie his own flies, but as the hooks were so difficult to find—and he didn't have money to buy them anyway—he often took flies from his father's box. He undressed them and then re-tied them his own way, a thing that his father always pretended not to notice.

Eventually the war finished, and a needle factory near Valmaggia, a small Valsesia village, reopened, and he started making his hooks from sewing needles. The silk he also used came from a local manufacturer, Faro. They manufactured a three-ply silk, that was ideal for tying flies. The thread was split for tying small flies—even going to half a thread for very small flies—or left whole for bigger or more bulky flies.

In his early years, he also bait-fished quite a bit. He always used a hollow cane rod, and he alternated the traditional Valsesiana technique with a tech-

At eighty-three years old, Arturo Pugno, the master, needs no polarized glasses to spot fish. Sesia River, Italy. *Mauro Mazzo* nique that had a dead fish mounted on a hook. The advantage of the hollow rod was that it floats, and that's very useful when fishing for big marble trout with dead fish. You might need to throw the rod in the water to avoid breaking the line if you caught a big fish.

One day, his fishing life changed forever. He was sitting on the bank and saw a wagtail losing a feather on the river surface. The current carried it for a while, modifying its shape, and eventually, at the end of the pool, a big grayling came

Arturo's three-fly leader setup.

up and took it. He says he doesn't know why the grayling took it, but he decided he was going to fish with feathers as much as possible.

So he got addicted to the Valsesiana technique, where the flies are made of silk and feather. When he says silk and feather, he means only silk and feather, because he finds natural material far superior to any synthetic.

What is the Valsesiana technique? It is often confused with the Japanese tenkara, but it is quite different. First of all, the Valsesiana has no mysticism nor exotic rules. The flies are tied to catch fish and nothing else. They have to match the insects that the fish are feeding on. There are no right or wrong flies to use, and the most successful fishermen—thanks to experience—know which fly to use at which moment. If they do not have it in their box, they will tie it on the river bank.

He has spent all his life fishing with a cane rod. No, not the fancy rods made by Leonard and Payne. The cane he uses is not split *Arundinaria amabilis* from China. His rods are made with the hollow culm of *Arundinarieae Fargesia* robusta, similar to the ones used for bait fishing, with a special wood tip. To get an idea of how important the raw materials are, the rod tip has to be cut under the right moon, with only a few days in winter right for the cutting.

Along with his cane rod he carries all he needs for a day fishing in a leather wallet, where he has a repair kit for his horsehair fly line, and a complete fly tying kit (without a vise because he has never used one).

The tippet was also made of horsehair, because it is stiffer than nylon and makes for a better presentation of the fly. Using a stiffer leader, when it's properly manipulated, presents the fly as the first thing that the fish sees—the diameter of the tippet has little influence. Another advantage is horsehair doesn't have the disturbing refraction of nylon.

Arturo believes in the superiority of natural materials when it comes to fly fishing because every material is present in nature—like feathers or horsehairs, these materials are familiar to fish. These days Arturo uses nylon for his leaders, but never too small in diameter nor too soft because he believes it spoils the presentation.

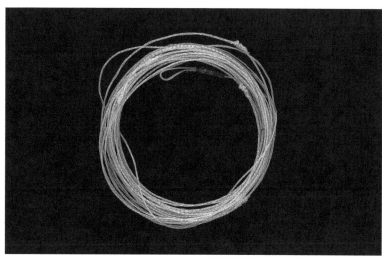

Arturo's horsehair line.

I think he also does some treatment to make it less shiny, but I never managed to get too much out of him on this. He says that telling too many personal techniques isn't helpful—a good fisherman has to think with his own head, not slavishly follow what other people say.

Arturo uses only two materials in his flies: silk and feathers. Laser hair dubbing, ice fiber, 3D synthetic quill—none of this exists in his world. His world isn't as small as it seems, though; talking to him you discover that there is more variety than you would think. The choice of the right feather, the movement it makes in the water, and the right shade and thickness of the silk thread is what he plays with.

And with his simple flies, he nearly always catches more fish than anyone else.

He ties flies with lots of different silks and feathers, and then prepares what he calls a "cast." His cast consists of a point fly and two to four dropper flies knotted on a leader. Each cast is placed in a cardboard sheet folded in two. On the cardboard he writes the hook number, the silk and feathers used, the line diameter, the length of each dropper, and the distance between them. He takes with him a few casts—the selection dependent on the season and the water. He also carries a bunch of feathers and silk threads, so in case he doesn't have the fly he needs, he just sits on a rock and ties a new one.

The same applies when he loses a fly: he reads the materials list on the cardboard and ties a new one. Going back to the car to get spare stuff has never been an option for him. Thanks to his knowledge of the places he is fishing, he manages to carry in one wallet all that he needs to fish and make small repairs.

His approach is quite different from that of the modern—and overloaded—fly fishermen, carrying hundreds of flies on the river and always complaining they are missing the right one. This happens because they do not carry a selection made for that river and season, only what the guy in the shop told them to buy. The more they carry, the better they feel.

To tie his flies, Arturo relies on materials whose origin is no farther than ten miles from his hometown. He has a huge supply of natural silk he bought in the 1960s from a local manufacturer, and it is the only kind of thread he uses. The feathers come from birds, either shot by himself, by friends, or picked up as roadkill.

The first thing Arturo tells you is that different feathers have different actions in the water. For instance, a feather from the neck and one from the chest move differently once underwater. Another important thing to remember is that the feather's colors change with the seasons.

To show the importance of the dressing, Arturo told me a short story. On one of his best days ever he caught nineteen grayling in less than two hours. He still remembers the day vividly, and his eyes light up when he talks about it. He fished this pool three days prior with little luck. He caught only a couple of grayling, so he went home and tied a bunch of new flies to try. The day he went back, he tied one of his new flies on the point and started catching them one after the other. Nineteen fish in less than two hours!

He was very happy, but he couldn't consider himself a good fishermen unless he was able to understand why this fly was doing so much better than any other. The fly had a light brown silk body, and the collar was tied with only three turns of a rush feather, taken from the neck, and not from the chest. The feathers from the neck are softer, and this, added to the very sparse collar, made the fly go a few inches under the surface, thus making it easy food for the grayling. Fish always prefer easy food.

Conversely, when fish are taking on the surface, you have to use feathers from the chest, because they are stiffer, and dry more quickly. You also have to have more turns with the hackle, in order to obtain a dense collar.

One of his best flies—a fly he uses when fish are feeding on live insects on the surface—is tied making the body with feathers instead of silk. He makes the body with woodcock fibers that are wetted and turned around the hook shank. Then he makes the collar with the same feather.

Another particular thing he does when we wants to improve the buoyancy of the fly is to make the collar by anchoring the hackle fiber by the tip. He then wraps it around the hook shank, and the fibers will make a bubble that traps air. This is a very complicated concept to explain; it's something only Arturo does. Coming off the center of the hackle you have fibers that are opposite one another. Normally when you wind a hackle you let the fibers lay opposite to each other around the hook. Arturo folds all the fibers on one side first using spit, and then turns them around the hook shank, and this creates a bubble.

Arturo makes his line from male horsehair sections, braided together, and then knotted. Usually he makes the thicker section with eighteen or twenty hairs, and then goes down gradually to two or three for the thinner sections. The line is composed of eight to ten sections, and the balance among them is very important—the line has to be powerful enough to be cast into the wind, but also delicate enough to guarantee a gentle presentation.

There are different styles of braiding the hairs, and Arturo believes the best is to braid all the hairs together at once. For instance, if he has to make a section consisting of sixteen hairs, he twists them all together. Other people braid the line differently, twisting two sections of eight hairs each, and then twisting the two sections together.

The line made his way is very adaptable. If you do a couple of strong false casts, it will trap a lot of air, and float better. On the other hand, if you want to make the line sink, just let the line absorb water during the drift and cast it very smoothly so as to keep the water in the line.

Arturo has fished all his life this way—getting the most from a very limited array of materials. If we would use more of our brains and less money from our wallets we would go further. Arturo, along with many of the great fisherman I had the fortune to meet in my life, always insists on one concept: Experience is the best tool of the fisherman. That's a life lesson in my view.

THE FISHING LIFE

A Different Soft Hackle Fly
Yvon Chouinard

Tying Arturo's soft hackle flies is not complicated, but properly tying these simple sparse patterns requires some thought.

Begin by attaching Pearsall's tying silk behind the eye of the hook. Smoothly wrap the silk down the shank to the bend of the hook and back to the eye.

Tie in the hackle by the tip with the base of the feather facing back over the eye. Next wind two turns of hackle backwards and tie off. Arturo uses very soft hackle feathers from moorhens, coot, starlings, or roadkill of various birds.

Wind the silk back behind the hackle and using pressure from the tying silk, force the hackle fibers forward Kebari style. Wind the silk back and forth, building a tapered body. You may want to dub a sparse thorax or tie in a strand of peacock herl. Wrap the silk back to the bend and whip finish. His colors of silk are olive, yellow, tan, brown, purple, and rust.

Arturo's soft-hackle fly.

CHAPTER 1
Trout and Their Food

YVON CHOUINARD, CRAIG MATHEWS, AND MAURO MAZZO

It does help to know the usual behavior of your quarry.

– The O'Dell Creek Gang

Trout's needs are simple: easily accessible food, cold clear water, and shelter from predators like otters, mink, humans, and many fish-eating birds like ospreys, herons, and pelicans. The various species of trout act somewhat differently from each other. Not only do they occupy different parts of a river, they are active at different times of the day, eat different foods, spawn in different places, and are fooled into taking different artificial flies fished with different techniques. We speak in generalizations here, but it does help to know the usual behavior of your quarry.

Rainbow trout live in the fastest currents, cutthroat trout in quiet eddies behind snags, brook trout in the pools at the inner bends of streams. Marble trout, bull trout, and other char are in the deepest pools. Small brown trout will be in slightly slower water than rainbows, and big brown trout will be in even slower water, tucked into cutbanks or in front of or behind boulders where they can lie in wait to ambush baitfish. Lake trout will cruise the lake edges right after ice-out or in the late fall. At other times, they live in the deep bottom of lakes.

These places are their normal lies where they feel at home and secure. They move to other parts of the river in floodwater, low water, when the water is warm or very cold, when there is a hatch, when they are resting or sleeping, in bright light, low light, and at night.

In high water, fish migrate to the banks to stay out of the fast currents and to take advantage of the worms, beetles, ants, and other terrestrials being swept into the river by the floodwaters. If the water is very dirty, they position themselves right next to the bank, a rock, or the bottom in order to keep their equilibrium. In warm water, they move to the deeper cooler waters or place themselves near a cool spring or tributary. Alternately, they could be under the fastest turbulent cascades where there is more dissolved oxygen.

After hatching, young trout (fry and parr) dart back and forth feeding on plankton, diatoms, and algae. As they become larger, they

OPPOSITE: Emerging blue-winged olives (a type of mayfly) land on a reel in the Henry's Fork of the Snake River, Idaho. *John Juracek*

PREVIOUS SPREAD: Bull trout rest after a long migration. British Columbia. *Steven Gnam* transition to feeding on insects, which they require for growth. At this stage, when they are less than six to eight inches long, most species of river trout occupy similar territories in the river and display similar behaviors. When they become larger, they begin to occupy their preferred lies in the stream.

When a hatch begins, the trout move from their secure resting lies into more productive water. It can be shallow riffles where the nymphs are emerging or next to foam lines that concentrate and transport food. They jockey around to be first in line without getting their tails nipped by a big boy. The larger, more aggressive fish have the best feeding stations; ideally, these will also be their more or less permanent lies.

Larger trout, sixteen inches and up, begin to exhibit even more different behaviors according to their species. These large fish need to eat more than tiny mayflies. They need the calories afforded by salmonfly nymphs, grasshoppers, crustaceans, baitfish, mice, swallows… ducklings. Brown trout transition to feeding on this larger food base sooner than rainbows.

THE FISHING LIFE

Seeing the Light
Craig Mathews

Last December, a couple moved to town and stopped by the shop complaining about having to wait several months before they could fish dry flies. I told them to get a fishing license immediately and a couple of midge dry flies and head down to the Madison River to fish trout rising to midges. They made their purchase, and I drew them a map of where to find surface-feeding trout.

A rainbow trout rises to a mayfly. *Barry and Cathy Beck*

A week later, they stopped back in and when questioned admitted they'd been on the river three days and had yet to see a fish rise but did have some great nymph fishing. Our winter guide, Dan, was tying flies that morning, and I asked him to take the couple to the river and show them some rising trout. The couple drifted back in later that same day and sheepishly told me Dan "showed us the light!"

They told me they walked to the river and stood while Dan sat on the bank and asked, "Do you see the rising trout?" Both thought Dan was kidding them until they too sat down and watched. Simply sitting on the bank put their eyes on a level with the surface of the river: The subtle rises to tiny midges became evident. Dan told me later, "You should have seen their eyes bug out when they saw all the fish coming to the surface."

Dawn patrol: Streamer fishing for fall-run brown trout on the upper Madison River, Montana. *John Juracek*

The Quarry

BROWN TROUT

Big brown trout, unlike humans, learn from their past and have a reputation for being smarter than other trout. They are shy, selective, wary, and not easily fooled. Browns like undercuts and overhanging banks and brush, boulders, rock cliffs, and deep pools. They are very hard fighters and often jump when hooked, then take off on bulldogged runs into the depths of the river or lake.

They are most active in low light or at night, when they can leave their secure lies to maraud around the shallows and pools looking for smaller fish. In the middle of a bright day, they become very picky eaters. A dry fly must be perfectly presented and drifted with no drag, and it might take a good emergence of mayflies, caddis, or stoneflies to bring them to the surface.

RAINBOW TROUT

Rainbow trout are the acrobats of the trout world; when hooked they take to the sky. There are several species of rainbows that occupy a wide range of habitat from large, roaring mountain rivers to tiny spring creeks. Rainbow trout are some of the hardest-fighting fish known to freshwater anglers. If rainbow and brown trout are present in the same river, anglers often catch more rainbows because they occupy water more easily fished: riffles, pockets, and pools.

CUTTHROAT TROUT

Cutthroat trout display behavior more like brook trout than their rainbow trout cousins. They are most often found in quiet current tongues along undercut banks, under rock ledges and deadfalls, and in slow, deep pools.

The cutthroat is often easily fooled, and its curiosity about big, bushy flies with bright colors and tinsel is legendary. They like to chase their prey and are suckers for large, rubber-legged dry flies slapped on the water and twitched. They have a reputation for being easy, but during a pale morning dun emergence they can be the most selective feeders, focusing on only one stage of the mayfly.

Cutthroat trout fight stubborn and hard along the bottom of the river or stream. These fish need cold water and prefer solitude, making the best fishing for them a chore, but worth every bit of the effort.

GOLDEN TROUT

The most beautiful of all trout, the golden trout is more than just golden in color; it also has various shades of lavender, pink, blue, yellow, and red.

They live above 10,000 feet in the streams and lakes of California, Alberta, Montana, and Wyoming. In the high-altitude lakes, they have a reputation of being picky eaters, probably because they feed mostly on tiny chironomids (midges).

MARBLE TROUT

Marble trout (and bull trout) are baitfish eaters. The marble trout is the biggest of the trout species and can pass the fifty-pound mark. They live only in Europe on the rivers of the Adriatic Basin. Marble trout are considered an endangered species, and environmental groups in both Italy and Slovenia are making strong efforts to restore their population. They are a very wary fish, and their preferred habitat is deep and fast water. Marble trout feed mainly at night; dawn is the best time to fish for them. Streamers are the first choice, followed by a nymph and a dry fly.

BROOK TROUT

The brook trout is a species of very cold waters in the high country, or mostly northern climes. It is a foolish fish and naïve compared to the brown and rainbow trout. It is a stubborn and strong fighter, and one of the most beautiful fish in the world. Brookies occupy tiny brooks, streams, beaver ponds, and lakes. It has been successfully introduced into the Patagonia region of South America where it occupies large rivers and bocas, and may reach several pounds.

Brook trout are easy to fool, and are found in places on most rivers and streams that are easily reached: big pools, soft riffles, along undercuts, and under overhanging trees. Mostly though, they are found in soft, deep water, tend to feed lower down on the water column, and are less likely to take surface flies.

GRAYLING

Grayling like water with medium to slow current, a gravel bottom, and a depth from one to four feet. They like clean water, but they also like feeding on gray water drainage, as experienced by Yvon when he fished for them in Italy.

Grayling live in schools; when you find one, persist in your efforts because there will be others around. They are mainly bottom feeders and are the main quarry for the Czech nymph technique. But when a hatch starts, they immediately switch to insects on the surface. When fishing them with the dry fly, try to avoid drag as much as possible; graylings are very spooky fish. Fishing them with nymphs is much easier because they are not wary of human presence and you can get quite close. Fish them on a short line to have greater control of your fly.

The Food

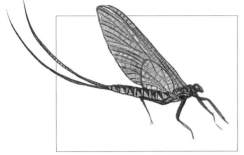

MAYFLIES

Mayflies are perhaps the best-known insects to anglers and are very important in the diet of trout. They spend all but a few days of their lives underwater and are available to fish all year long. These insects inhabit every trout stream and the sheer number of species in any stream is often amazing. But the list of those responsible for most angling opportunities in an area is short, usually not more than a dozen.

Emerging mayfly nymphs reach the surface in several ways. Some escape their nymphal skeleton at the bottom of the river or in the water column, with their wings trapping a gas bubble to buoy them to the surface. Others form gas bubbles inside their nymphal shuck that brings them to the surface; still other species migrate to the shoreline to hatch. As a mayfly hatches, it moves and shakes its nymphal shuck in an attempt to escape, causing the shuck edges to shimmer.

The freshly emerged insects are called duns, and even though trout take far more nymph mayflies during the year, there is nothing more visible and dramatic than a trout feeding on duns on the surface.

A day or two later, the insects return to the water to mate and reproduce. They molt and shed their dun skins, becoming sexually mature, and are now called mayfly spinners. Spinners return to the water and lay their eggs, then die on the surface, providing one last period when trout can feast on them.

When fishing mayfly hatches, first learn what stage of this insect the trout are feeding on. If mayfly duns are on the water and fish are rising everywhere, first watch the naturals float over rising trout. If trout let the duns pass, the fish are most likely rising to floating nymphs and emergers. If you see trout tails, it is likely nymphs are being taken under the surface. If you see noses, heads, and backs breaking the surface or fish taking the duns as they drift over, the trout are obviously taking duns. If you note casual, unhurried rises with a slow spreading rise ring and hear a soft kissing sound made by the fish as they take insects, then the trout are likely rising to mayfly spinners.

The strongest mayfly emergences usually take place in inclement weather conditions. Cloudy, cool weather is best; misting rain or snow is ideal. The best fishing during mayfly hatches is on days when the weather is poor because there are more insects than on bright, sunny days, and insects ride the water longer in cool weather and suffer more hatching defects that do not allow them to quickly escape the surface of the water. Too, trout seem to feel more comfortable feeding under overcast skies, so you can approach and cast to them more easily.

Conversely, mayfly spinners. important to fly fishers, all require warm, calm weather to lay their eggs. Cold, windy weather with any precipitation does not allow spinners to reach the water.

The stage when nymphs hatch into adults, in and under the surface of the water, is when the wet fly works its magic. Fishing a wet fly imitation on the swing—across and downstream—is a deadly technique when fishing for trout taking emerging mayflies.

The most common imitations of mayfly nymphs are Pheasant Tail, Hare's Ear, and March Brown Nymphs. These flies are also excellent searching patterns. If during a hatch you see fish tailing, try these patterns unweighted and fished just under the surface.

Mayfly nymphs are usually fished dead drifted and without motion. A few still-water species are good swimmers, and anglers usually fish imitations with a short strip retrieve.

The best dry fly mayfly emergences are those in which insects are clumsily escaping their nymphal exoskeletons and riding the surface with their nymphal shucks attached. These mayflies trigger good rises of trout because these insects are impaired—trapped in their shucks—and cannot easily escape.

Trout rising to mayfly spinners always rise much more casually and will take spinners in thin water and quiet pools nearer the shoreline. These rises will be quiet takes, merely sips.

First learn which stage of mayflies the trout are feeding on. Get as close to the rising fish as possible. Count the trout's rise rhythm; if it is feeding every four seconds or fourth natural insect floating by, then put the fly on his nose in four seconds or inline with the naturals.

CADDISFLIES

Caddisfly hatches often baffle anglers, as they are the insects least understood by fly fishers. In his book *Caddisflies*, Gary LaFontaine notes three clues indicating a caddis emergence. The first is trout seen leaping in the air when they chase emerging caddis pupae to the surface.

The second clue is there are no insects on the water. Even during a heavy caddis hatch adult caddisflies are nearly impossible to see drifting on the surface; they emerge and fly off unnoticed. The strongest clue to a caddis emergence is that no insects are seen on the water and yet fish are rising like mad.

Third, expect to see fish bulging and splashing in fast water, or quiet dimples, porpoise rolls, or tails breaking the surface in slower sections of the river.

> Other than knowing where the fish are, it is most important to know what they are likely to be eating.
>
> *– The O'Dell Creek Gang*

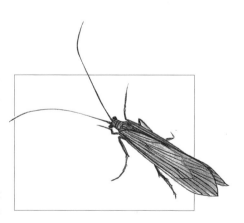

Caddisflies have a three-stage life cycle: larva, pupa, and adult. The transformation from larva to pupa is much like a moth caterpillar spinning a cocoon and later hatching into an adult moth.

Caddis emerge when a gaseous bubble forms inside their pupal skin, causing them to shoot from the bottom of the river, lake, or stream toward the surface. They also experience emergence problems as they emerge subsurface and often become entangled in their pupal shuck. Caddis mostly emerge in the afternoon or evening, so by getting close to the rising fish, you can keep track of your cast and the fly as light conditions fail.

Several clues indicate caddis hatches. Early in the hatch, small trout will be seen leaping out of the water as they chase emergers to the surface and their high-speed chases carry them out of the water. There will be no insects on the water, since the adults quickly fly off or scuttle to the shoreline grasses. When larger trout rise to caddis emerging in faster currents, you will see bulges or splashes. In slower flows, there will be quiet dimples, slow, porpoise-like rolls, and tails barely breaking the surface.

Caddis pupae are most available to trout when they hatch from pupae to adults. Most swim toward the surface and emerge there, while other species of caddis drift some distance with the currents. In both instances, trout easily capture them, and it is during this time fishing a wet fly or soft hackle on the downstream and across swing is deadly.

Caddis nymph imitations offer a choice between larvae and pupae. Some species of caddis are important to anglers fished as larvae. Larvae are not swimmers, so the pattern is best fished dead drifted near the bottom of the river or stream.

For the larvae, an excellent searching pattern is the Peeping Caddis, which very often is a favorite point fly and deadly for most of the season.

For the nymph imitation, there is the whole family of Czech nymphs patterns, tied on a grub hook weighted on the back to avoid snagging on the bottom, to choose from. They are excellent searching patterns and can be fished any time of the day, in medium to fast water.

At the beginning of a hatch, trout feed on pupae on the bottom, and one of the best flies is the LaFontaine Bead Head Caddis Pupa, fished close to the bottom. As the hatch goes on and pupae come to the surface, it is worth trying to cast an unweighted pupa imitation, such as the LaFontaine Emergent Sparkle Pupa, downstream and let it swing and add a twitch once in a while.

Caddis emergences are strongest in late evening into complete darkness. Get as close to rising fish as possible to keep track of your fly as the light fades.

A few caddis species offer good dry fly fishing opportunities when females lay their eggs. Look for caddis bouncing on the water, trying to break the surface tension, or for spent caddis on the surface of the water, on boulders, or on your waders. Female caddis might use these as well as overhanging brush and grasses to access the water to lay their eggs. Remember that even though female caddisflies move a lot while laying their eggs, a dead-drift presentation is always more productive.

Rarely will rising trout be selective when taking emerging caddis. But since caddis emergences can be heavy at times, it might seem that your fly can't compete with all the naturals on the water. Here, short, quick, and accurate presentations increase the chances your fly will be taken. A favorite method for taking big trout rising to emerging caddis is to present the fly just upstream of the rising trout, and as the fly approaches the fish give it a jerk with a short pull, causing the fly to be pulled under and then pop up again in front of the rising trout.

STONEFLIES & SALMONFLIES

A stonefly's life cycle consists of two stages: nymph and adult. The majority of a stonefly's life is spent in the nymphal stage (from one to four years); as adults they only live for several weeks. Several days prior to transitioning into adults, the nymphs migrate toward the shoreline to leave the water and emerge.

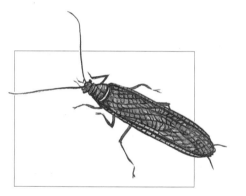

Stonefly nymphs can be very important to anglers as most species crawl out of the water to emerge. Some stonefly nymphs are quite big, up to one and a half to two inches, and the most common place to fish them is fast-flowing streams. Imitations are very often heavily weighted, and one of the most effective ways to fish them is to cast the heavy fly no more than fifteen feet upstream, let it sink, and follow the drift, first lifting and then lowering the rod tip.

Prime dry fly fishing occurs when female stoneflies return to the water to lay their eggs. Egg laying often occurs in the afternoon and evening hours. There is no doubt when trout are rising to adult stones. Aggressive, swirling, splashy rises can be seen as trout hurl themselves into overhanging brush to chase the adults.

One thing you should keep in mind when fishing dry fly adult stoneflies is flexibility. If a dead-drifted presentation fails, try giving your fly some movement, or pull the dry imitation under and let it pop back up to the surface just upstream of the trout, or sink it by trimming the wing off for a slimmer profile.

MIDGES

Midges are any of a number of small insects. And because midges emerge all year, these tiny insects should be at the top of your list.

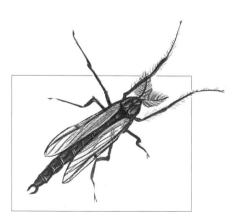

Midges emerge in the surface film and are susceptible to emergence difficulties, resulting in impaired and crippled adults caught in their shucks and trapped in the surface film. Rises to the naturals are casual and confident as the trout recognize that the insects cannot escape the surface.

With one exception, there is nothing unique about a trout's rise-form to midges. The strongest clue to a hatch of midges is adult midges are seen skittering on the surface or clustered along the shoreline where the trout are rising. The exception is big trout might be seen slowly bringing their entire heads out of the water like a periscope these will always be big trout rising to midges.

Trout must expend as little energy as possible when taking tiny insects like midges; they simply cannot afford to use up more calories feeding than what they ingest. Because of this, trout hold just below the surface when taking midges. Here, they will be extremely sensitive to wading waves, and if spooked, they will take longer to resume feeding than if they were feeding on caddis or mayflies.

On rivers, pupal imitations—the Starling and Red Soft Hackle most likely imitates emerging midges—dead drifted in the surface film work well. When fishing them in lakes or calm-flowing rivers and streams, slowly strip the pupa across the paths of cruising trout. When midge pupae float in the surface film prior to emerging, they swim away from an approaching trout.

A tenkara rod is ideal for winter midging. With no guides or reel to freeze up and fish that do not fight as hard as they do in summer, it is perfect for presenting a fixed-length, pinpoint-accurate cast every time. When we have only an hour or two of daily fishing and each cast can make the difference, tenkara allows the most efficient presentation, as well as hooking, landing, and releasing each trout quickly.

DAMSELFLIES & DRAGONFLIES

Both damselflies and dragonflies are important to fish and fishers. They thrive in almost all still waters, from large lakes to tiny ponds. Their nymphs are far more important than adults to anglers as they are available all year long in still waters.

Damselfly and dragonfly nymphs crawl out on shore to emerge and expose themselves to trout as they move from their weeded homes to the shoreline to hatch. The nymphs are ineffective swimmers and very vulnerable during these migrations, and trout prey ruthlessly on them. If you see fish quickly dart in knifelike moves at the surface or along the shoreline, they most likely are coming to damselfly nymphs migrating to shore to emerge.

Keep in mind that the nymphs of both insects always migrate in a line perpendicular to the shoreline, so imitations must be fished this

way, the way trout are accustomed to seeing the naturals. The imitation to use is made with a single marabou feather, in dark green or brown, wrapped around the hook shank to form the tail and the body of the fly. Fish it with a long leader, a few inches under the surface, and retrieve it very slowly.

When trout rise to damselflies, you often see them launch out of the water after the fluttering adults. Adult damsels are available to trout only during mating times or when afternoon winds kick up. When anglers see trout leaping out of the water to chase damsels, this is the clue to try a dry fly imitation.

If the fish ignores your offering, give it a twitch or a short pull on the next presentation. Try twitching or skittering the fly or even pulling it under and letting it pop back up to the surface to sit for a minute.

TERRESTRIALS

Terrestrials is a term that refers to ants, bees, beetles, grasshoppers, and the like. There are no hatches and no nymphs or other stages of aquatic life. Most terrestrial fishing does not involve concentrations of insects as you find when fishing emergences of mayflies or caddis. Sunny, warm, and windy afternoons are always best for grasshoppers, crickets, and mating swarms of flying ants. Beetles and ants also prefer warm, sunny days, but we've had great success using them all year long, even in winter.

Trout rising to flying ants, moths, crickets, bees, and grasshoppers will be noisy and aggressive, whereas rises to beetles and nonwinged ants are subtle, deliberate, and slow.

Flying ant swarms always bring tremendous rises of trout. In late summer, anglers should always be prepared to fish a mating swarm of ants. All trout relish ants and will rise aggressively to them. You will see big trout rising, taking several naturals quickly, like gluttons, before moving on and coming up a few feet beyond.

Terrestrial fishing may require doing whatever it takes—slapping the fly on the water or skittering or waking it on a tight line using drag to move the pattern. Terrestrial fishing does not usually involve heavy concentrations of insects, so anglers must cover more water in search of patrolling trout or cast to undercuts and cover, like overhangs. It is important to remember that trout move distances in search of terrestrials and might be in water where you might not normally expect them to be during other insect activity. Be aware of the water to the rear too.

CRUSTACEANS

Crustaceans include crayfish, scuds, and sow bugs, with the most important among them for the fly angler being scuds. Scuds are the freshwater equivalent of shrimp. They live in any water that has good weed

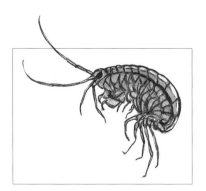

growth and vary in size and color. But like all shrimp, they contribute to the pink-colored flesh of the trout or salmon that feed on them.

If the trout in a particular lake are noted for their pink flesh, that's a good indication of the presence of scuds. If you pull up a clump of weeds, you will probably find lots of crawling and snapping scuds.

They are an important trout food and can easily be imitated by a simple pattern in an olive or tannish pink color. Fish the imitation by letting the weighted fly sink and then bringing it up with small, slow strips.

MICE & FROGS

Trout love protein, and mice and frogs offer up lots of it to huge trout patrolling the banks of rivers, lakes, and streams. Mice accidentally fall in the water and try to get out as soon as they can. Frogs live in the water but are wary of becoming trout food.

One simple rule must be followed: the fly must be presented along the shore and swim along it. Frogs and mice never swim away from the shore and out into midstream. Instead when disturbed, both critters usually jump into the water, then immediately swim or kick into the shoreline and hunker down until whatever disturbed them leaves. You can also try skipping the fly up onto streamside vegetation hanging over the water.

Big trout recognize this behavior and viciously strike naturals or imitations. While the action to mice and frog flies is usually not fast, it is always furious, so hang on!

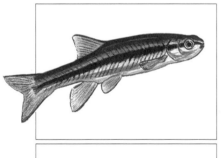

BAITFISH

Baitfish is a term that includes all the types of fish that are eaten by other fish. These include various kinds of minnows, sculpins, whitefish, suckers, and trout fry and parr. Trout are predators and will even eat the eggs and young of their own species. The largest trout are usually caught with streamers that imitate these baitfish.

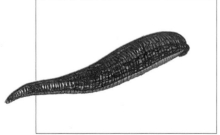

LEECHES, EELS, & LAMPREYS

If we had only one fly to fish with worldwide for trout, salmon, and bass—and even some saltwater fish—it would probably be the olive and black Wooly Bugger. God knows what it imitates, but the way it is normally fished, with slow undulating strips, results in it probably looking like a leech or eel.

Leeches come in a range of colors, including shades of brown, olive, tan, and gray. They swim by elongating and contracting their bodies in a smooth up-and-down motion. Wooly Buggers are usually weighted at the head to imitate that motion. Wooly Buggers can also be fished very effectively by casting one upstream and letting it dead drift in the current.

Techniques for Various Stages of Insects

STAGE	TECHNIQUE
Mayfly	
nymph	nymphing
emerger	wet, crippled dry, dry fly
dun	dry fly
spinner	dry fly
Stonefly	
nymph	nymphing
adult	dry fly, soft hackle
Caddisfly	
larva	nymphing
pupa	nymphing, wet fly, dry fly
egg-laying adult	dry fly
Damsel/Dragonfly	
nymph	nymphing
adult	dry fly
Terrestrial	
all	dry fly
Scud	
all	nymphing
Baitfish, Leech	
all	streamer, leech imitation

Mayfly Lifecycle

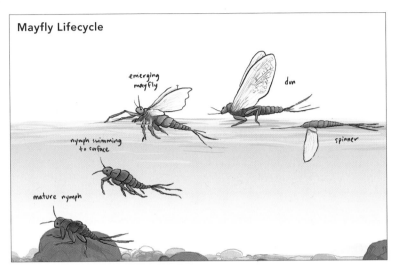

Caddisfly Lifecycle

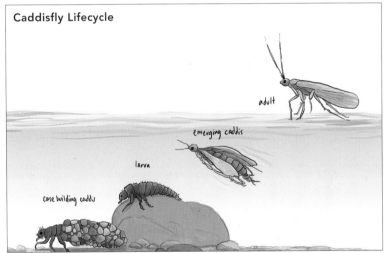

Midge Lifecycle

The Minestrone Hatch

Yvon Chouinard

First published in The Fly Fish Journal *(issue #4.2)*

During the 1960s, I spent summers climbing in the high Alps of France and Switzerland. When the weather turned foul, which it often did, we headed south for the sunnier Dolomites of Italy. If the weather followed us, we escaped to the topless beaches and limestone cliffs between Marseille and Cannes.

Driving through Italy, I never dreamed there could be fish in the rivers that tumble from the Alps. How could there be? These rivers were all dammed, diverted, channelized, polluted, and mined for gravel. I thought trout fishing in Italy must have suffered the same fate as hunting. Nearly every Italian male owns a shotgun but is reduced to shooting songbirds on their migration to and from Africa. They are plucked, impaled on a stick, drizzled with olive oil, and end up as uccelli carbon.

The Hotel Giardini pool on the Sesia River, Piode, Italy. *Mauro Mazzo*

Five years ago, I discovered I was wrong about the fishing. The streams of northern Italy flow through limestone, creating an alkaline environment (think San Pellegrino mineral water) that supports abundant insect life. I've found the fishing so good in Piemonte and Lombardia that several times I've had grand slams of rainbows, browns, grayling, marble trout, and marble brown hybrids. Now when I pass through Europe, I include a trip to the pre-Alps of Italy with my friend and rabid fisher Mauro Mazzo. The search is for trout, old Barolos, and the fabulous foods of northern Italy.

Driving through the Valtellina, the villages have sprawled so much that it's tough to tell where one ends and the next begins. One time, stopping to fish the Adda River downstream of the village of Chiuro, I was filled with doubt. Traffic careened along several major highways bordering the river, and houses, hotels, and restaurants lined the banks. Crowds of tourists filled the streets. But we were catching fish—fat, red-finned grayling up to two and a half pounds. I thought the fishing was great, but Mauro promised that about 2 p.m. the fishing would get even better. We moved up to a long pool with a sewer pipe coming in from the village. Promptly at two, gray water poured from the pipe, dishwater from lunches of bresaola, pizzoccheri, cheese dumplings, and polenta. A veritable soup of leftovers.

Tiny red worms crawled out of the bottom muck to feed on the minestrone, and the grayling went nuts feeding on the worms. Mauro gave me a small fly tied with only thick red thread wrapped around the shank. The world's simplest fly?

My tenkara rod stayed bent for the next two hours, until all the dishes were washed and it was time to recharge with an espresso.

THE FISHING LIFE

Deep Knowledge
Yvon Chouinard

We've heard a story about a young Native American fellow in Oregon who decided he wanted to become a steelhead guide. For a couple of days, he floated down the river with a mask and snorkel observing where the fish were. He immediately became the best guide on the river. What he observed in a couple of days would take years and millions of casts to learn in the normal way.

Claire Chouinard swims with the sockeye. Adams River, British Columbia.
Matt Stoecker

CHAPTER 2
Fly Fishing with Wet Flies and Streamers
YVON CHOUINARD

I got hooked on fishing at six years of age when my older brother Jeff took me to the polluted (still is) Androscoggin River near our home in Lisbon, Maine. Jeff caught a ten-inch pickerel, secretly put it on my line, and made believe I caught it.

When I was seventeen, climbing in the Teton Mountains of Wyoming, I was watching the mountain guide and excellent dry fly fisher, Glenn Exum, teaching his son Eddie to fly cast. When he saw me watching, he yelled, "Come over here, son," and he gave me my first lesson in casting. That was the end of spin fishing with Super Dupers for me.

I've been a serial specialist in every sport I've done. I throw myself into one aspect of the sport, and when I reach 75 percent fluency, I get bored and go on to the next passion. With fly fishing, I started out with wet flies, at first getting tips from my climbing partner Joe Faint, who was a Pennsylvania wet fly fisher. Then I moved on to streamers, graduated on to nymphs, and finally got obsessed with "matching the hatch" on difficult spring creeks with tiny flies.

These days I think I'm better balanced; I try to use the appropriate technique for the conditions. Yet I hardly used a dry fly last season. I fished almost exclusively old-school soft hackles. Fifty percent of the time that I fish for trout, I fish with a tenkara rod. I do it not as a novelty, but as a truly effective way to catch fish.

I also fish the salt, but I am not much interested in chasing fish that weigh more than my new granddaughter. I once landed thirty-seven varieties of fish in Indonesia. I hate fishing from drift boats or flat skiffs, and I try to lose the guide whenever I can.

THINK LIKE A TROUT

Wet flies imitate either baitfish, leeches, swimming nymphs, or emerging caddis and mayflies. The crawling or dislodged and drifting

> I try to lose the guide whenever I can.
>
> – Yvon Chouinard

OPPOSITE: Yvon tied into a Railroad Ranch rainbow on the Henry's Fork, Idaho. *Bryan Gregson*

PREVIOUS SPREAD: A yellow mayfly, New Zealand. *Val Atkinson* nymphs and scuds are covered in the chapter on nymphing. Baitfish and leeches are in the section on streamers.

For catching sheer numbers of fish, the most effective technique imitates nymphs either dead drifting or swimming to the surface. This chapter deals with the nymphs that are emerging—swimming to the surface to hatch as duns and then adults.

A sixteen-inch trout is not going to get many calories from a tiny size 18 mayfly. There is a net gain of calories only if the effort requires less calories burned than is gained through the food. It doesn't pay for a fish to swim up from four feet down to nab a tiny fly on the surface, especially when there is a good chance the fly will have dried its wings and flown off before it gets there.

Trout are masters at putting out the least amount of energy to gather their food. When they are feeding on small insects, they need a large quantity (a hatch) to make it worth their while, and they position themselves so they expend the least amount of energy to take advantage of that hatch.

The surest deal for them is to intercept the drifting nymphs or the swimming nymphs that are going to the surface or are just under the surface as they are breaking out of their shucks. Another easy meal is crippled flies that are unable to fully emerge from their shucks. Dead adult spinner mayflies splayed out on the surface are also an easy meal.

What a fish sees. Note bubbles.
Matt Stoecker

Trout, of course, feed most actively during a hatch but can be enticed to fall for an artificial fly at any time if the fly can be presented with an enticing action close enough to its lie so it only has to move a little and open its mouth.

The technique described here deals with mostly imitating that emerger stage of the hatch. It is one of the oldest techniques of fly fishing but one that has lost popularity to the dry fly, streamer, and nymph. Yet it remains one of the most effective techniques for catching fish during nonhatch periods. The method was very simply described by James Leisenring in his book *The Art of Tying the Wet Fly and Fishing the Flymph*.

I always fish my fly so that it becomes deadly at the point where the trout is most likely to take his food, which is usually at or close to his position in the stream. Since my flies are tied to act lifelike and look lifelike, I fish them so that the efficiency of the qualities is at its highest when it nears and arrives before the trout for his inspection. This is accomplished by allowing a gradual increase in tension caused by the water flowing against the leader, causing the fly to lift from the bottom and rise with the hackles or legs quivering after the manner of the natural fly.

We begin by describing wet fly fishing with a tenkara rod. Not only is it the easiest way to learn to fly fish, but it is possibly the most effective way to catch large numbers of fish.

THE FISHING LIFE

Lessons from a Simple Fly
Yvon Chouinard
First published in Trout and Salmon, May 2016

In the various outdoor pursuits and crafts in which I've been involved—from mountaineering and whitewater kayaking to spearfishing and tool making—the progression from novice to master has always been a journey from the complex to the simple. An illustrator becomes an artist when he can convey his message with fewer brush strokes.

Fishing with a fly seems to have gone in the opposite direction: it has become a needlessly complex and expensive pastime where anglers choose from hundreds of fly lines, high-tech rods, and trout reels with drags that can stop a truck. We all know that palming the rim of a reel with a simple click-drag can stop any trout or salmon, but the industry has become dependent on building insecurity in the minds of the customers—if we aren't outfitted with the latest gear and au courant signature fly, can we really be enjoying ourselves? (I must admit that I, too, have multiple rods and reels and I've caught myself cursing the fact that I don't have the exact fly for that specific stage of that particular mayfly.)

More than thirty years ago, I was introduced to the original method of fishing with a fly first described in the second century AD by Claudius Aelianus. This form of fishing is still practiced in parts of Spain, Italy, and Japan, in addition to places where people cannot afford modern gear. I've adapted this simple tenkara style to the large rivers of the Americas with great success. The combination of the long tenkara rod (no reel) and soft hackle wet-flies has proven for me to be the most effective way to catch trout on a fly.

I used to fish the soft hackles with a brace of different flies. Then I started noticing that most times, regardless of the hatch, the fish took the Pheasant Tail and Partridge. If that was so, why bother with the other patterns? Why not see how far I could go fishing an entire season with only one style of fly?

Like most new ideas in fishing, this one had been thought of before by Arthur Wood—the great English salmon fisherman who used only the March Brown for a whole season and a Blue Charm for another. He caught as many salmon as before and in fact, found his success with either fly was hardly different. Art Flick, the Catskill angler and fly-tyer who wrote *The Streamside Guide to Naturals and Their Imitations*, ended up using mostly one fly, the Grey Fox variant. Jim Teeny has used only the Teeny Nymph since 1971. Some of the most successful salmon fishermen in Canada use only the Muddler Minnow.

My scheme was to use only one style of fly for all trout, salmon, and saltwater fish.

Years ago, the American angler George LaBranche considered the myriad aspects of using dry flies to catch trout and ranked their importance. The position of the fly on the water he ranked first. Second, the action of the fly. Third, the

A Bahamas bonefish. *Rhett Cutrell*

fly's size. Fourth and fifth, the form and color of the fly. For the way I typically fish with wet flies, I rank the fly's action as most important, followed by size and presentation. I believe most anglers place too much importance on form and color.

The Pheasant Tail and Partridge (PT) is a neutral fly that fairly imitates most mayfly and caddis. It probably has its roots in the time of Dame Juliana Berners in 1496 when she wrote a treatise describing the wet-fly patterns used in England at that time. Frank Sawyer, the river keeper on the Avon, has been attributed as the developer of the modern Pheasant Tail nymph. Some years before, George Skues was already tying a version of the soft-hackle PT.

My one-fly season began in the winter and spring of 2015 when I used the PT on the flats of the Bahamas and Cuba. Bonefish that have been fished heavily can get spooky. If they "blow up" when you strip the fly it's probably because they have seen too many shiny hooks, bright eyes, and flashabou. I tied saltwater PTs on size 6 and 8 weighted bronze-colored hooks. I used long hackles from the backs of grouse necks and tied on two at a time to give a bushier look. With a small strip, the hackles pulsate like a jellyfish or shrimp. This plain brown fly even worked on light sand bottoms where you would normally use a lighter-colored fly. I've since used the PT for many other saltwater fish.

Fishing for trout in the spring and summer in Wyoming, Montana, and Idaho, I fished a size 10 or 12 as an attractor. When a hatch came on, I would switch to the appropriate size. Regardless of the color of the naturals or whether they were mayflies, caddis, or stoneflies, the PT, in the proper size, out-fished the more exact imitations.

My wet-fly technique is simple. I cast forty-five degrees downstream and mend the line to slow the swing. When the line starts to straighten, I slowly lift the rod to straighten it even more. Once the line is straight, I give an occasional twitch with the tip of the rod. I'm trying to imitate an emerging caddis or mayfly swimming to the surface or struggling from its shuck. Nine out of ten times the take is right after the twitch. The flexible tip of the tenkara rod is perfect for imparting this subtle action. I've found that a proper twitch is the most difficult thing to master in swinging wet-flies. Almost everyone overdoes it. A big twitch will send a wave of slack down the line, giving time for the fish to eject the fly. Remember, you are trying to entice a take, not scare the fish. If you're getting bites but few hooked trout, it's either a small fish or there's slack in the line.

Modern fast- and medium-action rods are not designed to impart movement to the fly; they're built to cast heavy flies a long distance—usually beyond the fish. Add the typical 5- or 6-weight line and the line droop at the end of the rod prevents any sort of twitch transferring to the fly. The best you can do is lower the tip to the water and try to give the smallest hand-strip. When I want to use a rod and reel, I use a cane rod or a ten-foot 2-weight rod with a 1-weight line to avoid the line droop. I also tie knotted leaders because the increased water friction helps to straighten the line.

When fishing a brace of flies, I tie the larger fly on the point and the smaller on the dropper, keeping them about thirty inches apart. The two-fly system increases the friction further and gives a different action to each fly. I can't emphasize enough the importance of giving action to the fly. Like your house cat, fish are predators. Slowly pull a toy mouse across the floor and the cat will go into its predator stance. Stop pulling and give it a twitch—the cat pounces. It makes no difference if the mouse is gray or yellow. Grizzly bears and tigers love it when you run.

In early July, I applied my one-fly approach to the salmon of the Hawke River in Labrador. The flies were tied on size 10 and 12 low-water salmon hooks. Later,

After a five-minute lesson, nine-year-old Lola proceeded to land seventeen rainbows in a day and a half. Fall River, Idaho. *Jeremy Koreski* on the Haffjardara in Iceland I had similar luck. Most of the fish were grilse and I used the sensitivity of a ten-foot, 5-weight rod to give action to the fly. The occasional twitch with the hitched fly was especially effective at inducing a take in slower water. I wasn't trying to prove a point anymore; it was simply the most effective way to catch these salmon. I've since taken to hitching the PT for trout, which often leads to explosive takes.

In September, I had an opportunity to fish for steelhead for five days on the Babine River in British Columbia. On the first day, there was only six inches of visibility. It cleared to a foot on the second day, but I had no confidence that a fish would be able to see my small flies. I put on a sink-tip line with a big dark Intruder and caught one small steelhead.

On the third day, I still couldn't see my boots but the water was clearer and the parr were active in the shallow riffles, feeding on caddis and green drakes in the afternoon. I thought if the parr could see the tiny naturals then surely the adults could see my size 10 PT. Sure enough, I started catching some large steelhead. I even caught two sockeye salmon, which is unusual so late in the season and so far from the sea.

Conditions continued to improve and I switched to a floating line and a hitched PT. Even fishing behind other anglers who were throwing traditional gaudy steelhead flies, the PT was producing fish up to thirty-seven inches. Many times when using large rubber waking flies for steelhead you get boils but no takes. I believe this is because the flies are too large. Rarely do I get only a boil with the small flies. In this situation, I'm convinced it was the most effective fly and technique I could have used.

We think anadromous fish take flies even though they are not feeding because it's a memory from when they were parr and eating insects. If that's so, it would explain why a small fly works so well especially when there's a hatch. We humans think of ourselves as perpetual teenagers; maybe salmon and steelhead do, too?

In the late autumn and through the winter, when the only hatches happening are tiny midges and blue-winged olives, most American anglers stoop to throwing streamers and gross rubber-legged and plastic concoctions—outfits for a Barbie doll, as the writer Tom McGuane calls them. But midges and BWOs are active swimmers, and a size 20 or 22 sparsely tied PT fished on the surface with a tiny twitch can be as effective as any fly.

Am I going to continue using only one fly for the rest of my life? My tying table looks pretty brown and boring ... also, I feel the lessons have been learned. Action and size are more important than style and color.

Limiting options forces creativity. Fishing for a year with only the PT has given me deep knowledge about what to do with that simple brown fly and a deeper understanding of fish. It has taught me that choosing a simpler life doesn't mean choosing an impoverished life. Rather, simplicity can lead to a more satisfying way of fishing and a more responsible way of living.

Yvon Chouinard landing a spring creek rainbow on a tenkara, Las Pampas, Argentina. *Bryan Gregson*

Tenkara Wet Fly Gear

TENKARA WET FLY RODS

Tenkara rods, now made of carbon fiber and telescoping, are mostly made in Asia. In Japan alone, there are hundreds of models for fishing everything from six-inch smelt to salmon and sea bass.

For trout fishing in Europe, New Zealand, and the Americas, we haven't found an advantage to using a rod longer than eleven and a half feet. The rod should be a bit stouter than the very light and limber rods popular in Japan for fishing very small mountain trout. My favorite is an eleven-and-a-half-foot soft hackle model from Temple Forks Outfitters. They also make a ten-and-a-half-footer and an eight-and-a-half-footer for small creeks and young kids.

These rods have a two-inch length of braided line glued to the tip called the lillian. Tie a stopper knot in this if there isn't one. To extend the rod, work from the tip toward the butt. Grab the tip near the lillian with your left thumb and forefinger and hold the next section firmly with your right thumb and forefinger. Pull *gently* until the tip is fully extended and starts to pull the next section through your right hand. Be careful not to overseat and jam the sections. Repeat the process with each section until the rod is completely extended. To collapse the rod, work from the butt toward the tip. Start with your right hand near the top of the butt section and your left at the top of the next section of narrower diameter. Push your hands together and repeat until the rod is fully collapsed.

If there isn't a line holder on your tenkara rod, you can easily make one. The easiest way to make these is to use large paper clips and attach them to the rod. Bend the ends of the paper clips to about a forty-five-degree angle.

Tie one paper clip on about an inch up from the butt of the handle and another an inch below the top of the first section. You can use string or just rubber bands to hold the wire loops. The fly can be stuck in the cork when walking from spot to spot on the river. I also keep a rubber band around the first section to tuck the tippet under when there's no fly, or when the leader and fly are not the right length to hook into the cork.

TENKARA WET FLY LINES

Line choice depends on whether you are fishing nymphs, dry flies, or wet flies and streamers. For fishing wet flies and streamers, I prefer to use a light floating line for my rod. The floating line casts better in the wind than monofilament or furled lines and can handle heavier

Tenkara Rod with Line Holder

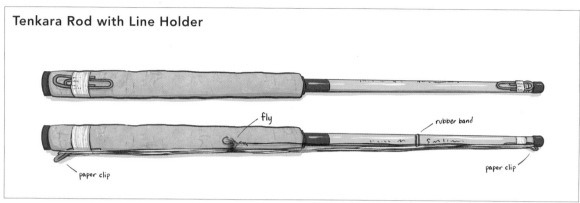

fly

rubber band

paper clip

paper clip

Extending the Rod

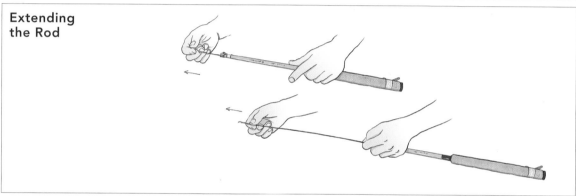

Rod Tip, Lillian & Stopper Knot

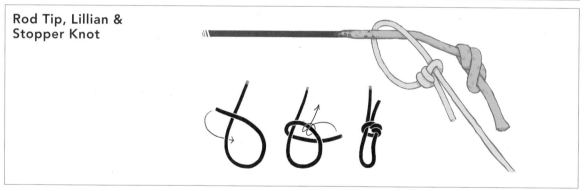

streamers. Since the line floats, it's easier to pick up and mend the line to control the speed and direction of the drift. Also having the line float is an asset in controlling the fly so it acts like an emerging nymph. However, even the lightest floating line may be too heavy to cast well on the more delicate tenkara rods.

You may be able to find a specific floating line for the tenkara rod. If you can't, don't worry as the lines are so short they do not need to be tapered. You have several choices. The easiest and cheapest way is to make your lines by cutting off the back end of an old weight-forward trout line, three weight or smaller. Or find a spool of running line that measures between .025 and .030 inches in diameter. Cortland (www. cortlandline.com) makes a forty-foot level line specifically for the Temple Fork rods.

For a ten-and-a-half-foot to eleven-and-a-half-foot rod, use a twenty-foot length for normal wet fly fishing and a twelve-foot length for small creeks or for nymphing. Also cut an eight-foot section to be used as an extender.

On the butt end of the lines tie a turle knot, leaving a one-inch long tag. Don't overtighten. Hitch the loop over the lillian and snug it down. The tag is for loosening the knot to take the line off the lillian. On the leader end, tie on a small loop (if there isn't one) using a nail knot, or tie a perfection loop.

TENKARA WET FLY LEADERS

I prefer to tie my own leaders partly because I don't like to spend four or five dollars for five cents' worth of nylon, but also because with a knotted leader you can use the knots to tie on multiple flies. The knots also create friction that helps to pull the line tight in the moving water so you maintain direct control over the fly.

The eight- to nine-foot tenkara wet fly leader is for swinging wet flies with the floating line. Tie a perfection loop on the butt of the leader, and tie together the sections listed below with a blood knot or surgeons knot. This should make about a nine-foot leader. Hitch the leader loop onto the line loop.

15 in. - .017 (20 lb. test) Maxima Ultragreen nylon
15 in. - .015 (15 lb. test) Maxima Ultragreen nylon
15 in. - .013 (12 lb. test) Maxima Ultragreen nylon
15 in. - .011 (0X tippet material)
15 in. - .09 (2X tippet material)
30 in. - .008 (3X tippet material)

Wet Fly Knots

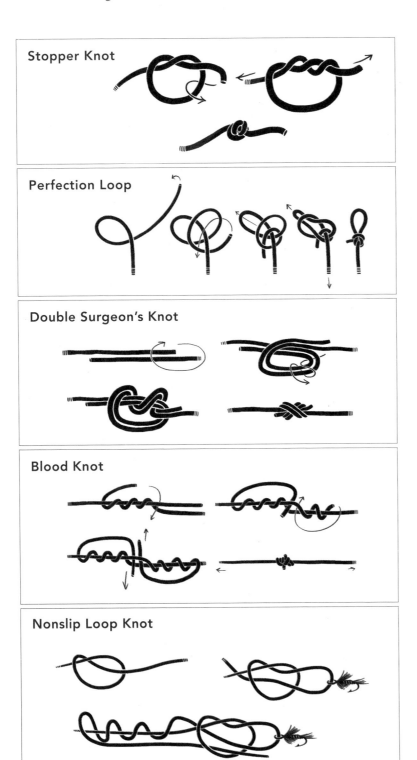

Stopper Knot

Perfection Loop

Double Surgeon's Knot

Blood Knot

Nonslip Loop Knot

Casting the Tenkara Rod

THE NORMAL CAST

The casting techniques are the same as casting a rod and reel, but it is much easier with a tenkara rod because the line is short, the rod is long, and you can keep your noncasting hand in your pocket.

I asked the great fishing icon and caster Lefty Kreh if he could describe how to cast a fly rod in just two sentences. He answered, "Easy, just do the forward cast as if you're throwing a spear. The back cast you throw the line behind you like you're throwing a Frisbee." To do that, you have to stand a bit sideways to the target.

All the rules of normal casting apply. Stand like on a surfboard or skateboard. Grip the handle with the thumb on top for wet fly fishing. For delicate dry fly fishing you may want to put your index finger on top for more sensitivity. Keep the rod tilted at about a sixty- to seventy-degree angle to the vertical. Use the core of the body for power like in tennis or throwing a baseball and follow Lefty's advice. Properly done, the line travel makes a small oval and is in constant tension.

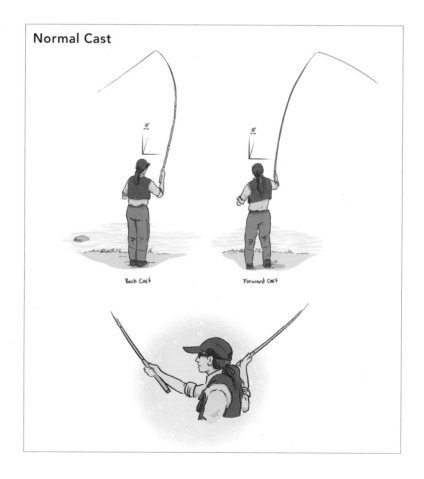

Normal Cast

Back Cast   Forward Cast

THE SNAP C CAST

This is a change-of-direction cast when there is no room behind you to back cast.

Place the rod parallel with the water with the taut line ninety degrees downstream. Draw a big C in the air with the rod tip, starting at the top of the C, and return it to the start position at the bottom of the C. Now the line is in the water, upstream of you.

Raise the tip to a vertical position. Go back slowly with your hand until the fly line is lying in the water close to your legs. Now start a forward cast like a regular overhead cast. Slowly punch it out.

Snap C Cast

THE BOW & ARROW CAST

This cast is done when there is no room to do any other cast. Use the shorter line that is slightly longer than the rod. Reach out and grab the end of the line with your nonrod hand and then grab the fly with two fingers. With the rod close to your body in front of you, point the rod at the target and pull the end of your line and the fly back to your ear, and let go.

Bow & Arrow Cast

Fishing Wet Flies with a Tenkara Rod

Start by tying a size 14 soft-hackle wet fly onto the end of the tippet using a nonslip loop knot (see page 57) or a clinch knot (see page 115).

Straighten your line and leader so there are no kinks or coils. This is important, as you don't want any slack in your system. I use a small piece of bicycle inner tube to do this by running the taut line through a tightly held fold in the inner tube.

Go to a riffle part of the stream where the water is from one and half to three feet deep with a current that's not too slow or too fast.

Wet Fly Fishing Techniques

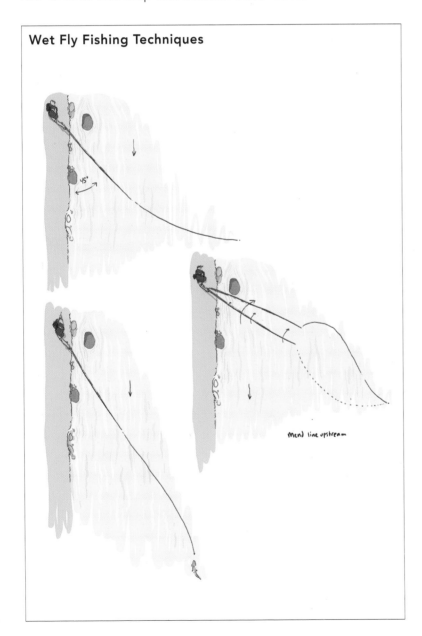

Cast the line at about a forty-five-degree angle downstream. As soon as the fly is in the water, lift the loose part of your line and place it across from you.

This mending upstream slows down the drift of the fly. Make sure you don't overmend and pull the fly out of the water. By mending upstream, you are trying to avoid the loose line getting caught by the current and swinging your fly across the current at an unnaturally fast speed. It also gives time for the fly to sink.

With your rod at about a twenty-degree angle to the water, follow the line with the tip of the rod. As the line tightens, lift the rod tip up to about a thirty-five-degree angle. As soon as the line comes tight, make an occasional twitch with the tip of the rod. It is important that the tip of the rod moves only two or three inches at most, no more.

To do this, hold the rod with your thumb on the top of the handle and your upper arm held straight down in a totally relaxed position (easy on the rotator cuff). The twitch is imparted to the tip by squeezing the bottom fingers of the hand, not by raising the rod.

If you look at your hand while you are doing this, you hardly see any movement at all. Almost everyone who tries to do this twitch overdoes it at first. Here's the rule: If you think you're not moving the fly enough, move it less. The key is to work only the top foot and a half of the rod. The rod itself hardly moves.

What you are trying to do is imitate the emerging and swimming stages of the caddis or mayfly. This is the stage where they are most vulnerable to a trout. As a result of the twitching action, the soft-hackle fly is going up in tiny increments of one to three inches. It is quite different from swinging traditional wet flies across a current.

In the seventeenth century, this subtle action of the tip was considered so important that the poles were made with a different, more flexible wood, or even ivory, for the last foot or eighteen inches of the rod.

With a good tenkara rod and the proper tip flex, you have such a direct control of the fly that you can make a caddis dry fly hop around on the water. Trout, steelhead, and salmon do not prefer to attack dead-drifted wet flies and nymphs. Just like a house cat or a grizzly—any predator for that matter—they want action. They want the type of action that imitates emergers, diving caddis, swimming nymphs, or wounded minnows. The best way to imitate that type of action—and to trigger a response—is to use a tenkara rod with a delicate tip and a tight, light line.

Most of the time, a fish will take the fly right after a twitch, whether you are using a waking fly for steelhead, a wet fly for salmon, or an egg-laying caddis for trout.

After each cast, take two steps downstream and cast again. Use the tension of the water against your line and fly to load the rod. One back cast and your line is back in the water. Do not false cast unless it is necessary.

When there are obstructions like trees or a cliff behind you, do a roll cast or a Spey-style cast like a circle C or double Spey to change direction and get the line out. Another advantage of the floating line is it is easier to do these casts, especially if there is a wind.

LANDING A FISH

When you hook a fish on tenkara gear with this tight-line method, the take is often violent. All that stands between you and the prize is the line and that long, flexible rod. With light tippet make sure you never point the rod at the fish; otherwise the tippet may break. For most trout, you keep the tip up and fight the fish using the flex of the rod. Connect with a bigger, hotter fish, though, and you'd better start running. When your only drag system is your feet, wearing good wading boots is critical. In extreme cases, you can always throw your rod in, strip off your clothes, and swim after it like Eddy, the fishing goddess in *The River Why*. The trout will swim away downstream, and feeling the pull of the rod gone, the trout will turn back upstream and head for its lie. The rod will swing downstream of the fish and tire it out. It may take a while, but good things come to those who wait. Often, you can grab your rod handle as it travels past, trailing after the fish.

After a fish is ready to come in, raise the rod up until you can grab the line with your free hand, tuck the rod under your arm pit, and haul it in hand over hand. Sometimes a big fish in heavy water just doesn't allow you to grab the line. In that case, collapse the rod (from the butt section) until you can grab the line.

Most of the time, you won't need a landing net if you fish a barbless hook. When you get the fish within reach, take your forceps and clamp them onto the hook and work it free of the fish. Avoid touching a trout, but if you need to, grab the lower lip with thumb and first finger and release it via the forceps.

ADVANCED TENKARA WET FLY TECHNIQUES

I generally fish the wet fly method using two flies. I consider this an advanced technique because unless you have the casting perfected you will end up with a horribly tangled leader. With two wet flies, and especially casting two weighted nymphs, if you back cast and forward cast with the line in the same plane, you will end up with a mess. It is important that you have the Belgian cast perfected.

If you try to use the normal overhead cast to throw two or more flies you will eventually end up with a tangled mess. The Belgian cast avoids the backward and forward cast traveling in the same plane and the quick stops of the overhead cast, the two things that tend to tangle lines. To do the Belgian cast, hold the rod at a forty-five-degree angle for the back cast and come more vertical on the forward stroke. This makes a big loop keeping the flies apart. No quick stops. It's a very fluid cast.

Belgian Cast

45°

Back Cast

Forward Cast

The two-fly method not only gives the fish a choice of flies, but the two flies add more drag, thus helping to straighten the line and giving more direct control of the flies. However, the primary advantage of using two flies is that the point fly and the dropper will have different actions.

To tie on one or more dropper flies, leave about a six-inch tag on your leader blood knot. Make sure the tag is the heavier of the two sections that are tied together, and this will keep the mono from wrapping around itself. Tie the dropper fly directly to the tag.

Another option is called the speed dropper by some. Tie a two-inch loop with a double surgeon's knot. Then tie another double surgeon's knot halfway to the end of the loop. Then hitch the loop above the tippet knot. The double nylon of the loop keeps the drop-

Craig Mathews thankful he didn't have to take a swim. A not-to-be-named creek in Yellowstone country, Montana. *Tim Bozworth*

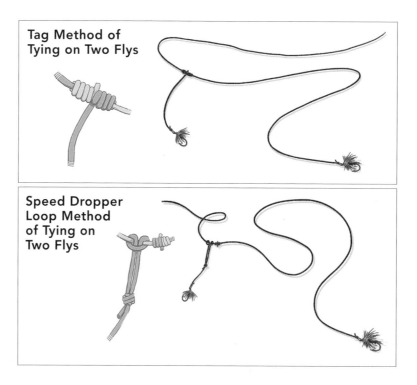

Tag Method of Tying on Two Flys

Speed Dropper Loop Method of Tying on Two Flys

per away from the tippet and can be replaced as the dropper leader gets shorter.

A typical two-fly setup consists of a point fly that should be the heavier or bushier of the flies. This is to add further drag to the line. Think of the point fly as being an anchor that helps straighten the line after the cast. A typical point fly would be a size 12 soft hackle on a 3X or 4X tippet, with a smaller fly for the dropper on a 2X or 3X tippet. The point fly can be about three feet from the dropper.

You rarely have to use very light tippet, because you're fishing downstream and the leader is not going over the fish. On spring creeks when the fish are wary and the hatches require small flies, you can drop down on your tippet sizing, but be warned you might get the line tangled, especially if there is a wind.

You fish two flies the same way you fish one: twitching and doing a lift at the end of the drift. Periodically, check your leader to see that you don't have a tangle or wind knot. A wind knot will reduce the strength of your tippet by 50 percent.

If you wish to sink the flies, use a smaller diameter tippet like 5X or 6X and cast farther upstream with slack in the line. If there is a fast current, throw a mend upstream to avoid the swing. If there is a slow current between you and the fly, do a downstream mend. When the line is straight downstream, you can twitch the flies and slowly lift the rod up. Don't be in a hurry to cast again. Leave the fly gently swinging on the surface for a few seconds. Think about teasing the fish. You will be surprised by how many times you can induce a take.

Hopping a Dry Fly on the Surface Using an Anchor Fly

If you wish to get down really deep, use a tungsten bead head soft hackle for the point fly.

If there are egg-laying caddisflies about, the advantages of a long tenkara rod and multiple flies can really be maximized. Start with a shorter line of twelve to fifteen feet. Extend the distance between the point fly and dropper to four to five feet. Put a Hare's Ear or Pheasant Tail soft hackle on the point, a fly that most resembles the caddis. On the dropper, tie on a dry caddis like an Elk Hair or Stimulator.

Cast upstream, across, or forty-five degrees downstream. At the end of the swing, lift the rod up until the dry caddis comes off the surface a few inches. Make the dry fly hop and skitter on the surface, imitating a female caddis trying to break through the surface tension of the water to lay its eggs on the bottom.

The trick to doing these little hops is extending the distance between the point fly and the dropper, and manipulating the last foot of the rod tip. Describing how to do it is like describing how to crack a safe. Just practice and you will figure it out.

You will know when you are properly fishing two flies. You will be hooking fish almost equally between the point and the dropper.

Things get really interesting when you hook two fish at once, which happens more frequently than you might think. For some reason, doubles are usually a brown and a rainbow. Browns are Republicans and rainbows are Democrats, and they never pull together. If they did, you would have a rodeo on your hands.

MAKING THE LINE LONGER OR SHORTER

Some tenkara rods made for larger US rivers are made stouter than the typical Japanese rods and they can handle lines up to thirty feet. To make a twenty-eight-foot line, put a turle knot on one end of your eight-foot extender (that you cut earlier from the fly line) and a stopper knot on the other. Hitch the extender onto the lillian, then attach the twenty-foot line above the stopper knot of the extender.

In a pinch you can shorten the line by tying a sheepshank knot. I first tried this on a small mountain stream in Montana. The fish were all concentrated in deep holes under logjams and cut banks and wouldn't come up for soft hackles or dries. I had on a twenty-foot line, which was too long for this creek and too long for short-line nymphing. I shortened the line to ten feet—so only the leader was in the water—using a modification of a sheepshank knot. I put on a heavy bead head nymph and proceeded to catch one to three rainbows from each pool.

Modified Sheepshank Knot

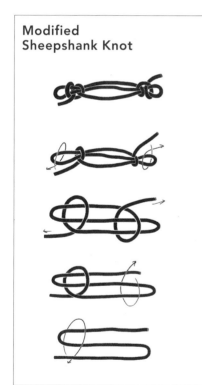

Line Sag

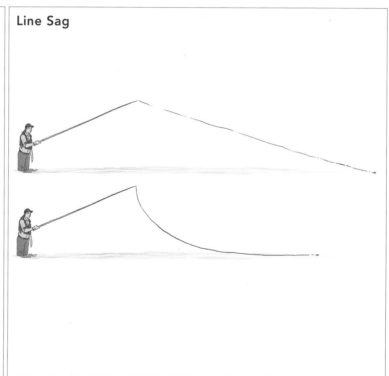

Wet Fly Fishing with Rod and Reel

You can somewhat adapt the tenkara wet fly method to a regular fly rod if you use a long slower-action rod. I recommend a ten-foot two-weight rod and underline it with one-weight line to avoid line sag. You cannot impart action to the fly if there is a sag or slack in the line, or if the line is being blown about by the wind. If you try to do the twitch with a fast action rod you will invariably over-twitch, as the whole rod will rise up. It would be better to point the rod at the water and give a tiny strip to the line with your stripping hand. Keep your casts short, no more than twenty feet, so you can better control the flies.

Press the line under your finger and just make believe you don't have a reel. Unless you hook a big fish, don't use the reel, just haul the fish in like you would on a tenkara rod.

In this kind of water there can be fish holding almost everywhere. Eliza Clayton fishes for western cutthroat on the North Fork of the Blackfoot River, Montana. *Noah Clayton*

Wet Flies

I have replaced all my traditional winged wet flies with soft-hackle flies. Since there is no top or bottom to the fly, there is never a worry that the fly is swinging on its side or upside down. I'll use a winged wet fly only if it is meant to imitate small baitfish rather than an insect.

Properly tied soft-hackle flies are almost impossible to find in most fly shops, but they are simple to tie, and I strongly recommend that you learn to tie your own.

I tie my flies with one important difference from traditional soft hackles: I tie most of them with a thorax made of Hare's Ice Dub. This is hare's ear fur plus a bit of synthetic glitter. This has two advantages. The thorax, which is tied after the hackle, keeps the hackles open so they don't lie against the body, and the sparkle in the dubbing, when wet, looks like the air bubble of an emerging nymph. It's similar to what a gold bead does to a nymph pattern. If there is no hatch I will start with a size 12 or 14 soft hackle as an attractor. When a hatch begins, I drop down in size to match the hatch.

WAKING FLIES

A very effective method for trout, steelhead, or Atlantic salmon is to drag a light fly over the surface, causing a small wake behind the fly. This imitates a swimming stonefly, water spider, or grasshopper. Use a soft hackle tied on a 2X light hook with a turned down eye. Insert the end of the tippet through the bottom of the eye and finish with a turle knot. With an upturned eye hook, use a clinch knot and do two half hitches with the tippet just in front of the hackle. These two methods will cause the fly to stay waking on the surface instead of being pulled down.

Careful to keep it in the water, Yvon Chouinard releases a trout on the South Fork of the Sun River, Montana. *Garrett W. Smith*

PARTRIDGE AND PHEASANT TAIL

In smaller sizes, this fly imitates the nymph or emerger stage of almost every mayfly; in larger sizes, it serves to imitate caddisflies or stoneflies. If I were to limit myself to only one soft-hackle pattern, it would be this one in size 14.

Hook:	#10 to #20 Dai-Riki #075 nymph 2X strong 1X short
Thread:	8/0 brown
Tail:	Pheasant tail
Body:	Pheasant tail
Ribbing:	Extra-small copper wire
Thorax:	Hare's Ice Dubbin peacock blend. To imitate a pale morning dun emerger, I use the lighter color Hare's Ice Dubbin hare's ear blend.
Hackle:	Partridge

MORMON GIRL

This pattern is a good imitation of the yellow sally (Mormon Girl) stonefly. You can tie other body colors using this recipe, including green, orange, and royal blue or purple.

Hook:	#14 to #18, standard wet or dry fly
Thread:	8/0 yellow
Body:	Yellow 3/0 thread or floss, double layer; red tag (optional)
Thorax:	Hare's Ice Dubbin hare's ear blend
Hackle:	Partridge

HARE'S EAR AND PARTRIDGE

STARLING AND RED

This is a good dark caddis imitation.

Soft-hackle flies can be very effectively fished during a midge hatch, as the pupa is a very active swimmer. Fish these with a tiny twitch to trigger a take. You can tie other colors using this recipe, including starling and purple and starling and rust.

Hook:	#12 to #18 Dai-Riki #075
Thread:	8/0 tan
Tail:	Tan Zelon
Body:	Light hare's ear dubbed
Ribbing:	Extra-small copper wire
Thorax:	Ice Dubbing hare's ear
Hackle:	Partridge

Hook:	#20 to #24, wet or dry fly
Thread:	8/0 black
Body:	3/0 red silk thread, wound double
Hackle:	Female starling

Fishing Streamers with a Tenkara Rod

When trout reach a certain size they change from eating small insects to eating large insects, like big stoneflies and grasshoppers, and leeches. Larger trout, four pounds and up—especially brown trout, lake trout, and char—want a square meal, and that means crustaceans, minnows, and even mice and lemmings. If you want to catch very large trout you should fish with streamers.

The tenkara rod can be used for fishing with flies that imitate baitfish, but only if the flies are small like some traditional wet flies or if they are unweighted, like muddler minnows. The tenkara is not so useful for casting large heavy flies. If you do get a take, it's difficult to set the hook because of the flexibility of the rod. Another disadvantage is that you cannot strip in line to give action to the fly. You will have to use other means that I will describe shortly.

You will need to use small lightly weighted streamers made of soft materials like marabou feathers. The current will make these flies pulse and dart like minnows. Because of the difficulty of setting the hook with tenkara, tie your flies with smaller very sharp hooks. Shorten your leader to six or seven feet total length with a 2X or 3X tippet.

A floating line will cast a heavier fly more easily than mono. Tie on a streamer using your favorite knot: clinch, nonslip loop, or turle. Cast the fly ninety degrees across the stream and mend the line downstream so the current will catch the floating line and accelerate the drift. Lead the fly with the rod and give an occasional twitch with the tip of the rod. What you are trying to do is offer a side view of an injured minnow to the fish. This is much more enticing than an end view.

Another way uses surprise to elicit a quick response. Let's say you have a large brown trout hiding under a bank on a meadow stream. Cast a large fly, like a muddler minnow, as close to the bank as possible, and slam the fly down hard and immediately pull it away with long twitches. Trout will follow the fly, and you may have to back up to extend the retrieve. If a large, smart trout gets too long a look at a large artificial fly he usually won't take. You want to elicit an instant reaction. What do you think would happen if you suddenly surprised a predator like a grizzly bear?

The technique of fishing streamer flies with a regular rod is not much different. You do have the advantage of being able to cast larger and heavier flies and use sinking lines to get down deeper where some fish hold. Also you can hand strip line in at varying speeds, giving better action to the fly.

Yellow is a good choice for streamer color when targeting autumn brown trout. Madison River, Montana. *John Juracek*

The Fish Should See the Profile of Your Fly, Not Its End

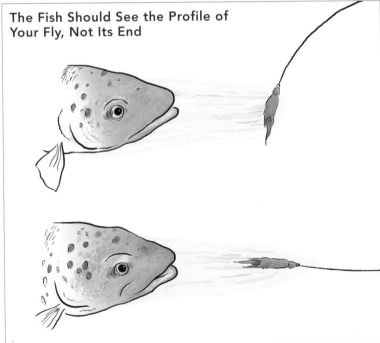

Recommended Streamers

Rather than an exact imitation, streamers should concentrate on mobility, motion, and sometimes a little flash.

With the slow action of light trout and tenkara rods, it's difficult to get penetration in the hard mouths of large fish. It helps to use chemically sharpened hooks with small barbs. Use the smallest-sized hooks in the longer lengths like 3X or 4X long. Don't go too long as the shank acts as a lever to pry the hook out.

A mouse fly caught this nice brown trout on a spring creek near Great Falls, Montana. *Nick Kelley*

THE FISHING LIFE

A Quick Study
Yvon Chouinard

I took a friend who had never fished before to a stream in Yellowstone where there were lots of aggressive pre-spawning browns throughout the riffles. I gave him my tenkara and a size 8 soft hackle. After a five-minute casting, twitching, and landing lesson, I left him alone. Since I had a regular rod, I fished behind him throwing long casts, covering a lot more water than he could with his twenty-foot line. At the end of the day, he caught more fish than I did, including a twenty-four-inch brown that slipped the hook right at his feet.

MUDDLER MINNOWS

This imitation can be fished dry as a hopper or wet to imitate sculpins. It's even a good salmon or steelhead fly.

Hook:	#8 to #12, Gamakatsu S11-4L2H or Dai-Riki #700
Thread:	3/0 black
Tail:	Mottled turkey quill, lacquered
Body:	Gold diamond braid
Underwing:	Gray squirrel tail
Wing:	Mottled turkey quill
Collar:	Natural deer
Head:	Natural deer

WOOLY BUGGERS

This fly can imitate eels, minnows, and damselfly nymphs. This version is a classic tie, but many variations are available in any fly shop.

Hook:	#8 to #12, Gamakatsu S11-4L2H
Thread:	3/0 black
Tail:	Black marabou
Weight:	Nontoxic wire wrapped around the front third of the shank, or use a bead head
Body:	Olive Krystal Flash chenille
Hackle:	Black palmered

SOFT-HACKLE STREAMER

This fly is simple, sinks quickly, and has lots of action. A good streamer for the tenkara rod.

Hook:	#8 to #12, Gamakatsu S11-4L2H
Thread:	3/0 red, white, yellow, or black; use a thread color that contrasts with the marabou wing
Tail:	Two strands of silver Flashabou or pearl Krystal Flash
Wing:	Blood marabou wound as a hackle. The most popular colors are black, olive, yellow, white, and black/olive. The wing is followed by a turn of mallard flank feather dyed to match the marabou.

CHAPTER 3
Fly Fishing with Nymphs
MAURO MAZZO

When I was a kid, I spent most of my time escaping from Grandma: I would go fishing with a can of worms. Those days, I was doing everything to come home with a few fish to show my grandma. I brought home a few things that were quite borderline; when the fish don't bite, you have to go find them.

Fly fishing in Italy in the 1960s was uncommon, and to be a fly fisher was a very posh thing. Most fly fishers walked the riverbanks wearing Barbour jackets while smoking pipes. They enjoyed talking about the best fly to match the hatch, asking themselves whether it was a dun with a gray body or a yellowish-green emerger—difficult stuff for a young kid.

When I was sixteen, the father of a dear friend of mine introduced me to the world of fly fishing. I was already fishing with artificial lures, mainly for trout and pike, with good results. I was afraid that fly fishing was more of a walking and talking exercise for older people than real fishing.

I took some casting lessons. The instructor told me that only when I had acquired the right casting tempo and made the decision to fish relying only on a bunch of hair and feathers, then and only then, could I consider myself a fly fisherman—or, as they called themselves, a purist. Being a teenager, I had an interest in beautiful hair, but of another kind, and no interest at all in purity, but I decided to carry on and see what would happen on the water.

The day came to go fishing. The teacher told us to find what insects were hatching and to tie on the right imitation. Nearsighted and without polarized prescription lenses, this was a little difficult for me. I couldn't see any difference in the insects; actually, I couldn't see any hatching insects at all. So I decided to tie on a fly with a red body, just because I liked it.

> The keys to being an effective fly fisher are: to know well the habit of the fish, and to be able to read the water.
>
> – *Mauro Mazzo*

OPPOSITE: Mauro Mazzo lands a good-size marble trout on a nymph, Sesia River at Piode, Italy. *Davide Badino*

PREVIOUS SPREAD: Fish on! Yvon Chouinard on the Sun River, Montana. *Garrett W. Smith*

Excited by the sight of rising fish, I forgot all the casting fundamentals; my fly plopped on the water, the line in loops around it. But on my second cast, I had a fish on.

A bell rang in my head. If I had a fish on after two poor casts, using a fly that I picked only because I liked the colors, fly fishing must be much easier than what the instructor told me—and also quite effective. I also realized that for nearsighted people like me, nymph fishing is the best option.

Today, after nearly forty-five years of fly fishing, I have not changed my mind. Fly fishing is simple and effective, and fishing with nymphs is still my favorite choice.

I have been lucky enough in my life to fish in many places around the world and for many different species of fish, from the moody Atlantic salmon to the mighty mahseer, from the elusive blue fin grayling to the ultrarare marble trout, and I believe that the keys to being an effective fly fisher are two things: to know well the habit of the fish you are trying to catch and to be able to read the water it lives in. Once you master this, even a bare hook can be the right fly.

FISHING WITH NYMPHS

For years, the subsurface fishing techniques were left to the days in which nothing else was working. The majority fished a nymph without any action, like a dry fly. They didn't know what they were doing. In the last few years, however, the opposite has occurred, to the point that nymph fishing has become like rocket science. Fly fishing competitions, no matter where they are held in the world, are almost always won using nymphing techniques

When experienced anglers talk about modern nymphing techniques, they like to use exotic names like Czech, French, or Spanish nymphing. These names only serve to confuse the beginner, who wonders what the terms mean and which one is best. Don't worry; the "best technique" does not exist. What's important is to use the proper technique for the water you are fishing. Don't worry about giving your fishing technique an exotic name—a "fast blue fish from the Baltic Sea" is still just a cod.

It is interesting to note that Czech nymphing started in Poland during the 1970s on the Dunajec River by fishers who were interested in competing. Fly fishing competitions were, and still are, very popular in the countries of what was formerly called the Eastern Bloc. The people had very little means, so they had to use what was available; they were fishing with no fly lines and no reels. They used only monofilament line and very simple nymphs, and as a result always fished the nymph very close to the rod tip.

Another peculiarity of this technique was that they used heavy nymphs so the nymph would sink very fast. If you think for a second, this is quite logical. If you cast a very short line, to get the longest possible drift in the feeding zone, you want to have your flies near the bottom, where the fish are holding, in the shortest possible time. Ironically, a technique that was born to overcome a lack of means has become a fashion in our ultra-affluent society.

The evolution of nymph fishing brought more than just fancy names; it also brought some interesting developments in technique. A bunch of innovative people revisited the old, well-known techniques and, by adding a few twitches, have made nymph fishing more effective.

Akin to fishing with a worm or bait, anglers fishing nymphs today often apply action to the nymph, thereby mimicking the wiggling worm or the swimming nymph. The most important things in nymphing are getting the fly to the right depth, achieving the right speed for its drift, and giving it some action to make it look lifelike.

Theories, like the one placing importance on the exact insect imitation, faded away, switching to techniques based on the presentation of the fly at the right depth and speed. Following this new approach, you will be able to fish more or less anywhere with only a few nymphs.

When can you fish the nymph? The answer will be disappointing. Always. Nymph fishing is not limited by an event, like a hatch going on; even in the middle of a hatch, fish are still eating mostly nymphs.

Additionally, fly fishing has a casting mystique that often frightens newcomers. Casting is definitely a nice thing, but it is just one of the tools you can use to make your fishing more effective. You will soon realize that most of your fishing can be done within twenty-five feet or less.

Most of us started fishing with a pole, a piece of line, and a can of worms. No one bothered to tell us how to cast the worm, but we caught fish anyway. Why? Because we were in the right place, at the right moment, presenting to the fish what it wanted to eat.

The important thing is the ability to choose the right place, go there at the right time, and fish it in the right way. Knowledge is the key. Every piece of water has one system that works better than the others, and our aim is to teach you to figure out what is the most efficient system for that particular place and time.

Tenkara Nymphing Gear

TENKARA NYMPHING RODS

The easiest way to learn nymph fishing is to start with a tenkara rod. The subsurface technique that best suits a tenkara rod is short-line nymphing. The tenkara rod, because of its longer length, is one of the best rods to practice this technique.

Considering you will often have to cast weighted flies, the most suitable action is progressive action that flexes most in the top two-thirds of its length, but not too soft. If the rod is too delicate and slow, it will be hard to set the hook.

TENKARA NYMPHING LINES & LEADERS

Lines for nymphing are made opposite of how they should be. Heavy heads buoy downstream with the current. Nymphing lines need to be thin and light. You are not fly casting; you are lobbing. You want to get the maximum control of the fly and thus the thin, light line. For short-line nymphing, use a twelve-foot line about .025-inch diameter. It need not be tapered.

The simplest leader is made of a four- to six-foot length of 3X to 6X tippet material. Tie a perfection loop on one end and hitch it directly onto the loop at the end of the twelve-foot floating line. If you don't have a very visible color of fly line, another choice uses an eight-inch-long piece of .011-inch-thick fluorescent yellow monofilament line with a perfection loop tied at each end. This will be your bite indicator. Hitch this piece directly onto the end of your fly line and tie your leader onto the other loop with a clinch knot.

The finer the tippet, the faster the nymph will sink, and the less it will be affected by the currents. Whatever leader system you are using, only the last few inches of the fly line or indicator will be touching the water. To improve bite detection, make stripes with black waterproof marker on every inch of the fluorescent section of the tippet.

Nymphing Leader with Strike Indicator

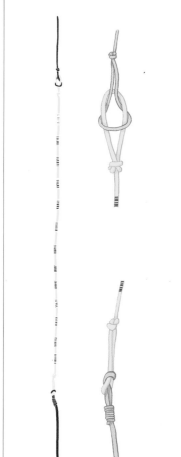

THE FISHING LIFE

The Fake Fly Box
Mauro Mazzo

A few years ago, Czech nymphing style was still unknown to most fishers. Sandrino, a friend of mine who competed for years with the Italian fishing team, and I booked a few days of fishing with Jiry Klima, the captain of the Czech fly fishing team. The Czech team was dominating the competition world at that time. We fished with him for several days and learned a lot. On the last day, we stopped fishing at about 6 p.m. and invited him for a beer at a bar right by the river.

Sandrino and I sat down still wearing our fishing vests, while Jiry went to the car and came back with a very nice wooden box, full of flies. "Sandrino, let's swap flies from our boxes," Jiry said as he came back in the bar. I thought it was very kind of him, but Sandrino didn't look too happy.

Jiry picked a bunch of flies from Sandrino's box and Sandrino did the same. After we had our drink and Jiry went away, I asked Sandrino why he didn't look happy about sharing the flies. He grinned. "They never give away their secret flies; I should have been prepared! The box he showed us was an ordinary fly

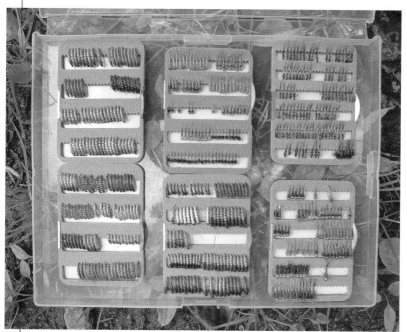

Several fly boxes of a well-known competition angler: secret flies or fakes?
Mauro Mazzo

box, whilst I showed him my competition boxes. So, he picked up some of my best flies, whilst I picked up his ordinary flies."

From that very day, I saw Sandrino swapping flies with many others. The box he pulled out was always the same one, though he had twenty more in his tackle bag.

Fishing Nymphs

FISHING A SINGLE NYMPH

When fishing with a single nymph, look for water with medium-slow current and a depth of two to three feet. Cast, relying only on the weight of the nymph, with a fluid arcing motion of the rod tip, forty-five degrees upstream of you. This casting technique is contrary to the traditional fly rod cast where the rod tip moves in a straight line and accelerates to an abrupt stop.

Another useful cast, especially when wading, is to let the line lay on the water behind you, and then cast it forward, using the tension of the water to load the rod. The movement is the same as an overhead cast, but without a back cast. You start with the line pulled taut by the current and cast your fly in front of you; the current dragging on your fly acts like a catapult.

The Water Tension Cast

Wait for a few seconds after the fly hits the water in order to let your fly get close to the bottom and then follow the nymph's path downstream with your rod tip. Try to avoid pulling the fly downstream. This is very important; the drift of the fly has to look natural. "Turbo-powered nymphs" swimming downstream faster than the current do not look natural.

But looking natural does not mean dead. If you want your fly to be effective, it has to look alive, and the best way to achieve this is to make little twitches with your rod tip during the fly's drift downstream.

These twitches have a double benefit: they imitate the movements of a nymph, and they can also trigger a reaction from the trout. In the wet fly chapter is an explanation about how to twitch your flies.

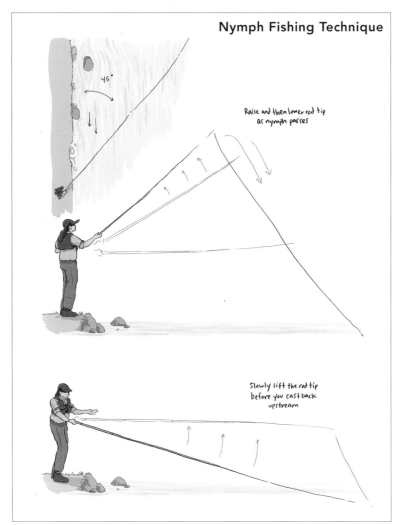

Nymph Fishing Technique

45°

Raise and then lower rod tip as nymph passes

Slowly lift the rod tip before you cast back upstream

I can only insist that the twitches be as small as possible. The slightest movement will be enough because the rod tip amplifies the movement. To keep direct control of the fly, keep as much line off the water as possible at all times, while also maintaining a little belly in the line to assure a drag-free drift. This is one of the most difficult things to learn because although you need to keep the line clear of the water, you do not want to pull the nymph during the drift and make it look like a hangman on a tree.

In between twitches, let your nymph drift free. I've found this combination of little twitches followed by a free drift the most attractive to fish. When the drift has reached its end and the fly starts to rise from the bottom to the surface, do not pull your fly out of the water immediately. The fish may think it is an emerging insect, and you may get a bite. Wait with the rod tip pointing downstream; sometimes the slow upward movement of the fly can persuade a doubtful trout.

You will need to develop a feel for the take. Some years ago a study was done with an expert fishing with nymphs in the old way by dead drifting the nymph on a slack line. An observer on a cliff above could see that on almost every cast a trout would take the fly and instantly spit it out without the angler even knowing.

We don't recommend large strike indicators that attach to the line. Beginners often use one to get a dead drift with a fly. We don't use them; we want direct control of the fly. You need to feel the contact and achieve a dead drift until you want to impart a subtle action when the fly is where the fish are holding. The strike indicator inhibits imparting that action, reduces take detection, and inhibits getting your fly down deep.

Fishing with nymphs, you need to determine how deep the pool is. If the pool is shallow or the current is slow, use a shorter leader and a light nymph. If the pool is deep or the current is fast, choose a heavier one.

You want to stay with the lightest possible nymph that will give you a drift speed close to the current speed. As a rule of thumb, the lighter the nymph, the better the drift. The problem is the drag on the fly from the leader and the tippet. You have to use a thin tippet and the lightest possible imitation to have your fly presented to the fish in the most natural way.

Once you have hooked the fish, keep the rod tip high during the fight, using the bend of the rod to fight the fish. To land it, reach out with your hand, grab the line loosely (the line has to be free to move inside your grasp to avoid breaking in case of a sudden run by the fish), and pull the fish in gently. Whenever possible, release the fish without taking it out of the water.

FISHING TWO OR MORE NYMPHS

Once you are familiar with fishing with one nymph, you can move on to the two-nymph rig—my favorite, particularly in medium-fast water. The two reasons for using two flies are to give the fish a choice of flies and to add more weight without having to use a larger fly. Make the tippet with the usual 3X to 5X mono, but add a six-inch dropper.

The distance between the dropper and the point fly should be about twenty to twenty-five inches; shorter in faster water, longer in slower water.

The easiest way to fish with two or more nymphs is to tie the heavier fly to the point and the lighter one to the dropper; this makes casting much easier. The most common rig is composed of a point fly, size 8 to 12 (weighted with a 3 to 4 mm bead head) depending on the strength of the current (the stronger the current, the bigger the fly), and a dropper with a fly of size 12 to 16 (weighted with a 2 to 2.5 mm bead head).

If you want to get the most natural presentation in slow current or with difficult fish, you can tie the smallest fly to the point. This will make the presentation more natural, but casting and bite detection will be much more difficult. For this reason, I suggest this rig only to people with a lot of experience. A good alternative for less experienced people is to use two small flies (14 or 16) of the same weight for both point and dropper.

The presentation is the same when fishing with two or more flies as when fishing with one. Because two or more flies are often used in fast current, you only need to change the angle at which you cast the fly to get the longest possible drift. The faster the current, the more upstream you will need to make your cast—up to ninety degrees in very fast currents. This is necessary to get a long enough drift for your flies.

You will have to make the action more dynamic. And you will have to lift the rod tip in the first half following the drift and lower it in the second half. The take will often be very hard, so detecting the bite in this kind of water is not that difficult.

How the two-fly nymph rigs work:

• Flies with same weight: The tippet drifts parallel to the bottom. This rig is good for exploring more water in the same drift at the same depth.

• Heavier point fly: The tippet drifts in a more vertical orientation. This helps when you want to explore two different levels of the water column.

• Heavier dropper fly: The point fly, in spite of its light weight, will run close to the bottom with a very natural drift.

Bhutan Brown Trout: Here Be Caddis

Yvon Chouinard

First published in The Drake, *Spring 2012*

In 1985, I was in Bhutan to climb Ganghan Puensum, then the highest unclimbed mountain on the planet. Our worthless Chinese and Indian military maps put us on the wrong side of the mountain, so we gave up and settled for making first ascents on some unauthorized 20,000-footers. We corrected the flawed maps and planned to tell our sponsors (National Geographic and Rolex) about our corrections. But standing around the campfire one day, we decided to burn our notes instead. There need to be a few places left on this crowded planet where "here be dragons" still defines the unknown regions of maps. Then I went fishing.

I knew that King Jigme Wangchuck was a fly fisher who had some spring creeks to himself, where he avoided wading by casting from atop an elephant. He was also married to two beautiful sisters and loved playing basketball. We watched a game in the capital city of Thimphu one day. The king waited under the basket (kings don't run) until the game came to him. When he scored, both sides cheered. It's good to be king in Bhutan.

Many of the rivers in Bhutan run clear and cold, and brown trout, introduced by the British, thrive there. Being at the same latitude as Miami, the insect life is prodigious. Some of the caddis cases I saw looked like small cigars.

Fishing near a small village one day, I was ignored by the women washing clothes along the bank next to me. Until I landed a pretty big brown. When I released the fish, the women began screaming, pounding me on the back, and indicating with fingers pointed at their mouths and bellies that they wanted to eat that fish. Their religion wouldn't allow them to kill the fish themselves, but if I killed it . . .

On another river, just outside Thimphu, the air reverberated with a deep Ohmmmmm coming from hundreds of chanting monks in the monastery nearby. I wasn't having much luck, so I sat on the bank, taking in the chants and searching my fly box for answers. I looked up to see a tall monk walking toward me. My gut cramped with fear. You are not allowed to fish within a mile of a temple, or monastery, in this strict Buddhist country, so I recognized trouble.

As the monk drew closer, I imagined myself being strung up in a dark dungeon of some sixteenth-century building. When he reached down and grabbed my fly box, I thought maybe I'd get by with just having my gear confiscated. Then he reached into the box, picked out a large gray nymph, and handed it to me. On the first cast, I hooked a fat twelve-inch brown and released it. The monk clapped and laughed from deep in his belly, just like the Dalai Lama.

Yvon taught this young monk to fly fish and gave him a rod when he left, Bhutan. *John Roskelley*

Nymph Fishing with Rod & Reel

Fishing with the rod only will oblige you to be very efficient with your fishing action. You can compare this to taking a picture with a manual camera with a fixed lens versus using an automatic camera with a zoom lens.

With a simple manual camera, you have only the aperture and focus to play with. Using a modern auto SLR camera with zoom gives you thousands of options, but unless you are a pro, you will not be able to fully utilize these options. You will take the occasional nice shot, but more often than not, it will be only by chance.

To master a craft, you have to achieve total control of the tool you are using. Photographers like Henri Cartier-Bresson, Robert Capa, and Elliott Erwitt made their masterpieces using only fixed lenses and manual cameras. Fishing is the same: learning with a very simple tool, with very few options available, will teach you how to get the best out of your tackle.

Once you have learned to fish without a reel, the transition to regular rod and reel will be quite easy. You will know from your tenkara experience that to catch fish you do not need to cast a mile. The ability to cast farther will be only an extra tool, not the foundation of your fishing.

If you are not a strong caster yet and are using a light nymph, you may want to add a butt section to your setup. Tie a loop in both ends of a three-foot length of .013-inch monofilament line, and hitch one end to the end of your fly line. To this hitch your fluorescent bite indicator with your tippet tied to the other end.

The ideal rod is a nine- to ten-foot progressive action one, meaning that the rod bends all through its length but gets stiffer toward the butt. The shorter option allows more precise casting; the longer one gives you better control of the nymphs during their drift.

The most important thing with the rod and reel is the balance of the rod. With most nymph fishing techniques, you have to fish for hours with your arm lifted to keep as much line as possible off the water. A well-balanced, light rod and reel will make your life a lot easier and will avoid that heavy tip feeling that makes you tire quickly. Use a large arbor reel, as it reduces the coiling of the fly line.

When fishing with nymphs, most often you will be casting weighted flies, so the lightest line you can handle is the best choice. When casting weighted flies, the weight of the fly helps you reach the distance you want (comparable to spin fishing), even though you are using a light rod and line. Conventional wisdom says you have to use

One of the world's greatest freestone rivers, the Madison, with its boulders and pockets, is ideal water for nymphing. Montana. *John Juracek*

a heavy line to cast heavy flies; you are supposed to load the rod with the weight of the line only. But this approach would oblige you to use very heavy lines, seven weight or more, and that would make it impossible to fish with the techniques described here.

I want to make it clear that to a nymph fisher, the only real advantage of a fly line and a reel is the ability to change the length of the line out of the tip and the ability to control that line. You can do short- or long-line nymphing. Apart from this, when nymph fishing, you will be better off using a monofilament line. The monofilament, thanks to its thin diameter, which is less than half of the thinnest fly line, is less subject to the action of the wind, which allows you to detect subtle takes. It is also less exposed to the action of the current, which facilitates a natural drift for your nymph. You don't need a separate spool for your reel loaded with monofilament. Just loop a forty-foot section of twenty- to thirty-pound monofilament shooting line onto the tip of your fly line.

When fishing with a light downstream wind, you can take advantage of the fact that the monofilament is half the diameter of the thinnest fly line, and you just keep your rod close to the water. When the wind is strong, if you keep the rod high you will make a big bow in your line that will drag your fly faster than the current. To defeat this drag, as soon as your fly hits the water, mend upwind and lay the line down on the water. Follow the drift with the tip of the rod, mending if necessary, and when the indicator stops strike sideways and upstream. In this situation, the use of a floating strike indicator will help bite detection.

The bare truth is that you don't really need a fly line, but to make casting easier when fishing very light nymphs, get the lightest line possible. For all-purpose nymphing, the ideal rod is a four weight, set up with a one- or two-weight line.

You need to adjust your casting to this peculiar rig. Reduce false casting to a minimum, because when using weighted flies, the only thing false casting does is increase the chances of tangling the leader.

Mauro Mazzo tight-line nymphing for marble trout. Sesia River, Italy.
Daniela Prestifilippo

As soon as the fly touches the water, you have to try to maintain contact with the flies. This is very important because the fish might take the fly during its descending path and you have to be ready to strike immediately. A good way to maintain contact with the flies is to keep the fly line under your index finger during the cast. When the fly hits the water, stop the line by pushing your finger against the rod handle and start retrieving the line using the other hand to take up the slack.

When following the drift of the flies, try to keep the rod tip close to the water and shorten the line using the left hand (when holding the rod with the right hand).

With rod and reel, you can make longer casts, but don't forget that this does not mean you are obliged to do so. The best fishing is often close to the bank, and being cautious and silent when approaching the bank will help you be successful.

A big advantage you get from the reel comes when fighting a big fish. The reel offers you the possibility to play the fish with ease, letting line out and retrieving it in accordance with the behavior of the fish. Please bear in mind that playing a fish for too long can overstress the fish.

THE FISHING LIFE

The Usual Question
Mauro Mazzo

I was fishing the Firehole River in Yellowstone Park while a big hatch was going on, and I was doing really well with two small nymphs, which I was fishing just under the surface.

I watched a young boy running up and down the river casting a big dry fly here and there, followed by his mother carrying a large landing net. I could tell he had no idea what he was doing.

He came by and asked me the usual question, "What fly are you using?" His mother explained that he was supposed to be hiking with his group, but all he wanted to do was fish.

I changed his rig, tying on a very simple leader, made of seven feet of mono, and tied on a nymph under a piece of yarn to be used as a strike indicator.

His casting was very basic, so I told him to cast very close to the bank, behind a rock that was hiding him from the fish. After a few casts, he had his first fish on. His eyes were sparkling, and I knew he was caught on fly fishing.

Tying Nymphs

My nymphs are tied very simply. These patterns are mainly searching nymphs, but they catch fish, showing once more that the exact imitation theory is not always right. The priority is to offer a fly similar to what the fish are eating at the right depth and drift. The weight of the fly, and its disposition, is very important; the dressing itself is more impressionistic than realistic. There are ultrarealistic imitations in the nymph world, but I have never seen them catch many fish. Their place is in a nice cabinet in your house rather than on the riverbank.

I believe that names are good with insects and dry or wet flies, but with most nymphs, apart from the famous ones, names are rather confusing. Maybe anglers don't feel it's very cool to tell people they fish only Pheasant Tails or Hare's Ears, so they give their flies exotic names like PT Cruiser, or Tollett's™ Half-Juiced. Rather than suggest fly X or Y, I will give basic information that will allow you to fish most waters.

For dark stream bottoms, use a dark fly; for light bottoms, use a light fly. For faster or deeper water, use a big fly tied on a size 8 to 12 hook, and weight it with tungsten bead heads or nontoxic wire. For slower or shallower water, use a small fly tied on a size 12 to 16 hook and weighted with a bead head or wire. For the smallest sizes (16 to 20), use 2X strong nymph hooks with no weight.

Bear in mind that with only ten imitations, tied on different-sized hooks, you can embark on a world fly fishing tour. With the nymphs I describe in the following pages, I have caught fish all over the world, from trout to steelhead, from Atlantic salmon to grayling. I believe they are all you need to cover 90 percent of situations.

SOME TIPS

The tips that follow are valid for all nymphs and will help you decide which flies to choose for your box.

• Use bent, or jig, hooks, weighted in the top or middle of the shank to reduce the chance of snagging flies on the bottom. This kind of fly is preferred when fishing rivers with an uneven bottom or one full of debris.

• A thin body makes the fly sink faster; a coarse, fluffy body slows down the sink rate. Use a thin body for fast water, a fluffy body for slow water.

• Silver or gold bead heads work better in colored water. Use brass, black, or no bead heads in clear water.

The Firehole River, Yellowstone National Park, Wyoming. *John Juracek*

CASED CADDIS IMITATION

Hook:	#10 and #12, jig, 2X long, 2X wire
Bead head:	Gold or black 3 mm
Tail:	Green or yellow fluorescent wool or floss
Body:	Hare's dubbing with a color that matches natural insects
Legs:	A couple of turns of partridge hackle

UNI NYMPH - LIGHT

Hook:	#12 and #14
Bead head:	Gold, 2 to 3 mm
Tail:	Partridge hackle fiber
Body:	Beige Hare's dubbing
Thorax:	Hare's Ice Dubbin peacock blend
Rib:	Copper wire
Collar:	Orange floss (optional turn of partridge hackle before the floss adds a lifelike effect)

UNI CADDIS LARVAE - LIGHT

Hook:	#12 to #16, grub
Body:	Beige dubbing
Thorax:	Dark brown and orange dubbing
Back:	Elastic vinyl, with five or six turns of nylon monofilament around the body keeping the back in place; also imitates a scud

UNI NYMPH GREEN

Hook:	#14 and #16, grub
Bead head:	Gold 2.5 mm
Tail:	Furnace rooster hackle fiber
Body:	Bluish-green Hare's dubbing
Collar :	Fluorescent orange floss

UNI EMERGER NYMPH - LIGHT

Hook:	#16 and #18
Bead head:	Gold 2 mm
Tail:	Gray hen or rooster hackle fiber
Body:	Light gray or beige Hare's dubbing
Thorax:	Peacock herl
Collar:	Hen gray hackle

HARE'S EAR

Hook:	#12 to #16, 2X long, 2X heavy
Tail:	Partridge
Ribbing:	Copper wire
Body:	Various shades of Hare's Ear
Thorax:	Hare's Ice Dubbin gray
Wing case:	Goose quill or magic shrimp foil
Hackle:	Partridge
Collar:	Orange floss (optional)

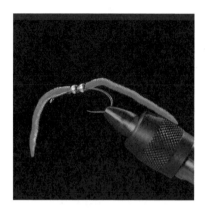

SAN JUAN WORM

Hook:	#8 to #12, grub, 2X long, 2X gape
Bead head:	Gold 3 to 4 mm
Body:	Red or pink chenille

SCUD

Hook:	Grub 14-18
Weight:	Non-toxic wire 0.15 (optional)
Thread:	Light gray 8/0
Body:	Seal substitute dubbing gray, or Antron dubbing
Back:	Pearl thin foil
Rib:	Silver fine wire, or nylon monofilament

BWO NYMPH

Hook:	Straight 14-18
Bead head:	Copper tungsten bead head 2.8 mm
Thread:	Tan 8/0
Tail:	Gray Hen or CDC fibers
Body:	Light green dubbing
Thorax:	Dark gray opossum or Hare's Ear
Rib:	Silver fine wire, or nylon monofilament

BLACK AND RED NYMPH

Hook:	Jig 12-16
Bead head:	Silver tungsten bead head 2.8 mm
Thread:	Black 8/0
Tail:	Coq de Leon fibers
Body:	Black floss
Thorax:	Peacock
Rib:	Silver fine wire
Spot:	Red fluorescent floss

BLACK PALÙ POLIFEMO

Hook:	Jig 8-12
Bead head:	Jig off bead head 4 mm
Thread:	Black 8/0
Tail:	Natural pheasant
Body:	Black floss
Thorax:	Pink Antron
Rib:	Silver fine wire
Spot:	Red fluorescent floss

LIGHT COLOR PERDIGÓN

The Perdigón fly is coated with a thin layer of UV resin (made by Solarex or Loon).

Hook:	Jig 10-16
Bead head:	Jig off bead head 2.3-2.8 mm
Thread:	Light tan 8/0
Tail:	Coq de Leon fibers
Body:	Light gray floss
Thorax:	Purple tinsel
Rib:	Light blue fine wire

UNI CADDIS LARVAE - DARK

Hook:	#8 to #12, grub
Body:	Dark brown or dark green dubbing with red spot
Thorax:	Peacock herl
Back:	Elastic vinyl, kept in place with five or six turns of dark nylon monofilament, or copper wire around the body

UNI STONEFLY NYMPH

Hook:	#8 to #10, grub, 2X long, 2X gape
Bead head:	Orange 4 to 5 mm
Tail:	Pheasant tail fibers
Body:	Pheasant tail fibers
Thorax:	Hare's Ear Ice Dubbin peacock blend
Rib:	Copper wire

UNI MAYFLY NYMPH

Hook:	#10 to #14, 2X long, 2X gape
Bead head:	Gold, 2.5 to 4 mm
Tail:	Pheasant tail fibers
Body:	Pheasant tail fibers
Thorax:	Hare's Ear Ice Dubbin peacock blend
Rib:	Copper wire
Legs:	Partridge hackle on top with V shape
Back:	Dark pheasant tail fibers
Collar:	Orange floss

UNI NYMPH JIG HOOK

Hook:	#12 to #16, jig, 2X long, 2X gape
Bead head:	Gold 2 to 2.5 mm
Tail:	Pheasant tail fibers
Body:	Dark brown Hare's dubbing
Thorax:	White Hare's dubbing
Collar:	Orange floss

UNI EMERGER NYMPH - DARK

Hook:	#14 to #18, grub, 2X length, 2X gape
Bead head:	Gold, 2 to 2.5 mm
Tail:	Furnace hackle
Body:	Greenish-brown Hare's dubbing
Collar:	One turn of gray hen hackle

SAWYER'S PHEASANT TAIL NYMPH

Hook:	#12 to #16, 2X long, 2X gape
Tail:	Pheasant tail fibers
Body:	Pheasant tail fibers
Thorax:	Copper wire
Rib:	Copper wire
Wing case:	Pheasant tail fibers

Nymphing for Anadromous Fish

There are times when nymphing techniques are the most effective way to fish for steelhead, Atlantic salmon, and sea trout.

• When the water is cold in the morning or in the winter when the fish won't move very far to chase a swinging fly.

• When steelhead are near spawning pink or sockeye salmon, they want to eat those eggs!

• When the water is warm in the dog days of summer and the salmon have gone dour.

• Whenever anadromous fish (for whatever reason) are schooled up in deep pools.

• When in Southeast Alaska and spring steelhead are often reluctant to take swinging flies and really prefer egg patterns.

• When fishing for hatchery fish who hardly know what an insect is. They want a fish pellet or smelly egg.

All anadromous fish are suckers for worms and gobs of cured smelly salmon eggs. In Iceland after the season closes, and the catch-and-release sports have left, the farmers go out with their cans of worms and catch their winter supply of salmon.

If you can see fish holed up in a deep pool, there is a good chance you can catch them—and sometimes every one of them. These big fish in deep water feel secure and are not spooked by lines, heavy leaders, or even humans standing ten feet away. The method is simple: drift a rubber-legged stonefly nymph pattern past their noses, and give a little twitch. The important thing is to get the fly down to their level so all they have to do is open their mouths and suck it in.

All fishers have their weaknesses; that's why we have a reputation for lying. There are times when no matter how skillful we are, we go through long periods when we can't catch a fish. Atlantic salmon, with all their neuroses, especially can drive you to drink. Steelhead are easy; they will take almost any fly, but there are so few of them left. In our desperation, we hear the siren songs of the scented egg or the heavily weighted Snelda or Red Francis, and we look jealously at the spin fisher tossing his sacks of Gooey Bob eggs and hoovering up fish

Jasper Pääkkönen releases an early season Atlantic salmon, Finnmark, Norway. *Juuso Syrjä*

after fish. You can avoid the temptation of the sirens with cotton plugs in your ears . . . or just pull out those nymphs.

It is an effective method, but it might not be everyone's cup of tea. It might be an alternative for those days on which endlessly swinging a fly is like watching the same movie five times and expecting a different ending.

A Tenkara Salmon

Yvon Chouinard

When Atlantic salmon first move into a river on their spawning run, they seem to be in a terrible hurry to get somewhere. They jump as they enter a pool and, seconds later, jump again as they leave it. It can be frustrating times for the angler, because the fish are not much interested in stopping to take a fly. Not until a day or two later when they settle down into a comfortable lie and out of habit, boredom, or to defend their spot, they may fall for a bunch of feathers on a hook.

ABOVE: *Malinda Chouinard*

OPPOSITE: Let's rodeo! Yvon Chouinard tenkara fishing for grilse in Iceland. *Malinda Chouinard*

Fishing in the Haffjardara River in Iceland recently we were blessed with a good run of grilse and small salmon. At the riffle area of the upper Aquarium pool, as a lark I decided to see if I could manage a salmon on soft-hackle flies and my twenty-five-year-old tenkara rod.

I put an eight-foot extender onto my twenty-foot floating line as I wanted to keep farther away from these spooky fish. I tied a Shakey Beeley onto the 2X tippet and a blue and partridge soft hackle with a red tag onto the dropper—both tied on size 12, upturned-eye light salmon hooks. On my second cast, right after I gave the fly a twitch, a five-pound grilse took the dropper. Surprisingly, it wasn't as difficult to land as an equivalent rainbow or brown trout, which after feeling the hook, tend to streak away immediately. I landed four more that day and lost twice as many for various reasons. One I lost was a large salmon that broke off in the Count pool when I panicked and failed to throw the rod for fear of losing it in the rapids below.

Later during the week, I landed a dozen more with a few in the seven-pound-plus proper salmon range. Three times I had to throw the rod in the river when I couldn't stop the fish on its initial run. To tell the truth, the first time it happened, the rod was actually ripped out of my hand. I ran as fast as I could in the waist-deep water but never could catch up to my waking rod handle. But after seventy-five yards, I saw my rod turn and come back upstream. I ran back up and caught up with it near where the fish first took the fly. Later, I started to notice a pattern in the fight. After the pressure is off, the salmon (like a large trout) wants to return to its secure lie. Its querencia. However, I don't recommend you try this craziness unless you have a good run out—the inevitable rodeo needs plenty of room.

CHAPTER 4
Fly Fishing with Dry Flies
CRAIG MATHEWS

When I was four years old, my parents started taking my brother, Tom, and me to Silver Lake near our home in Grand Rapids. We spent the summers there, and I learned to fish for bluegill and bass. Every evening, we'd watch three fly fishermen wade out into the lake and cast their bamboo fly rods. It was magic to see their fly lines cutting the evening air, and they would hook up often and bring to net big bluegill, crappie, or bass.

One night, I mustered the gumption to join in their fly fishing lineup. I took my grandfather's bamboo rod hooked above the wooden frame of our walkout basement door, opened the door, walked out, and promptly closed the screen door on the rod, busting about a foot off the end. Undaunted, I waded into the lake toward the anglers. One of the men, who lived in a log cabin nearby, motioned me over and gave me a short casting lesson along with a couple of small poppers and a rubber Spider Fly. It was only a few casts before I was into a four-inch bluegill. I took a few more that first evening and was hooked on fly fishing for life.

A few days later, we were driving home from grocery shopping and saw the same three men walking from a bridge into the woods not far from our summer place. My mom dropped Tom and me off and waited in the car for us. We snuck up on the men and found them rigging up their tackle at a pond in the forest. I'll never forget the fish rising to the surface of the pond that day. Not knowing what they were, we sat watching, and then approached when one of the men landed one—a brook trout with brilliant spots on its flanks. I was hooked again and began learning all I could about fly fishing for trout.

Later, after I graduated from college, Larry Dech and I headed west to fish Yellowstone country and its incredible fly fishing opportunities. Not long after, my wife, Jackie, and I came to Yellowstone in September to fish for two weeks. We returned home, and a month

> Fly fishing helps preserve our capacity for wonder.

– Craig Mathews

OPPOSITE: Craig Mathews on O'Dell Creek, Montana, with a nice brown that took a terrestrial imitation. *Mauro Mazzo*

PREVIOUS SPREAD: Craig Mathews works his magic with dry flies on the Madison River, Montana. *Patrick Daigle* later, we schemed to move to Yellowstone, which we did later that winter. I came as the police chief of West Yellowstone, and she was a police dispatcher.

A few years later, we opened Blue Ribbon Flies and began fly tying and fishing for a living. We fish over one hundred days a year and talk about it daily with our friends and customers.

Over the years, I went from fishing dry flies exclusively to solely fishing nymphs, then to streamers, and back to fishing dry flies again. There is nothing I enjoy more than watching a trout come up for a dry fly. I now fish dry flies over 90 percent of my time on the water, and I use tenkara rods 75 percent of that time. I enjoy its effectiveness, efficiency, and simplicity. There is nothing I enjoy more than to see a trout come up to the surface for a dry fly. For me the world stops when a big trout sips in my dry fly. I raise the rod tip, set the hook, and my only audience is the trout and me. It's magic.

Most fly fishers feel there is magic on our planet, and it is held in our rivers, lakes, and streams. Henry David Thoreau once said, "Many men go fishing all their lives without knowing that it is not fish they are after." Most of us sooner or later discover that fly fishing helps preserve our capacity for wonder. Pursuing wild fish with a fly rod can teach us to see, smell, and feel the miracles of stream life with the serenity and the beauty of nature all around.

FISHING WITH DRY FLIES

It's been four years since we wrote the first edition of *Simple Fly Fishing*. Since then we've discovered new-improved techniques, fly patterns, and ideas making our simple fishing even more productive, rewarding, and fun. We'd like to share them here with you in the revised copy of our book.

My favorite method of fly fishing is with the dry fly. I enjoy the visual aspect of it. I prefer the stalk and the hunt: I enjoy slowly patrolling the banks of rivers, ponds, and streams searching for the telltale ring of a rise, a trout's back or snout breaking the surface as the fish rises to a mayfly, caddis, or midge. To me, there is nothing more satisfying than getting as close to the rising trout as possible, whether slowly sliding along the bank on my butt or wade-walking in the river on my knees.

Before I arrive at my fishing destination I've done my homework. I know where and when to expect insect emergences taking the guesswork out of what flies I'll need. I also know the time I should arrive to find insects hatching and trout rising. This allows me to fish efficiently, effectively, and more productively. I'll catch trout with less time spent sitting or walking the banks in search of rising fish, all of which can cause frustration for the uninitiated.

A mating swarm of caddisflies, with the larger females fluttering and attempting to lure the smaller males. *Jake Hawkes*

If I do not find fish actively rising to insect activity when I arrive on a stream, I can usually find one or two coming to the surface if I am patient and "sit on water." By this I mean I locate a quiet pool, pocket, or slow run where trout hold and feel secure. I find a comfortable spot along the shore and sit, watching the surface for a telltale ring of a subtle rise or a fish's tail or dorsal fin barely breaking the surface. Then I go back to my old profession as a police detective to find the clues of what the river is telling me to do. Are there midges emerging or mayflies? Are there ants on the water? When I discover what is bringing the trout to feed on the surface, I knot on an imitation and begin my fishing day.

If I do not see a rise, I might tie on an attractor pattern, a fly that imitates nothing in particular but may entice a rise. I prospect with my attractor pattern, covering much more water than I normally would with rising trout. Often, the attractor fly moves a fish to come up and take a look at it without taking it. I then tie on a pattern that imitates an insect the fish are used to seeing—an ant, beetle, or mayfly I know could be active at that time—and present it.

My First Time with a Tenkara Rod
Craig Mathews

The first time I saw a tenkara rod was a few years ago on O'Dell Spring Creek near my home in the Madison Valley of Montana. Yvon had come to spend a

Yvon Chouinard fishes O'Dell Creek, Montana. *Tim Davis*

few days fishing with me. We arrived at the creek, and Yvon stowed the rod in the rear pocket of his vest, explaining that he and Mauro had fished the rod recently on a small stream in Wyoming and had had a fun day fooling cutthroat trout. I couldn't help smiling to myself as I followed behind, thinking about hooking and landing a huge spring creek brown trout on the delicate tenkara rod with a fixed-length line and no reel.

We both fished our traditional rod-and-reel setups that morning. After lunch, Yvon finally pulled out his tenkara rod and tied on a small Blue-Winged Olive soft hackle and proceeded to catch several nice browns up to fifteen inches.

I marveled at how efficient Yvon could be using short casts, swinging his soft-hackle flies in all the likely looking spots—undercut pockets and pools— where trout jumped all over his presentations.

When he offered to let me try the rod, I quickly knotted on a grasshopper fly and cast it upstream a short distance to the next undercut bank. A four-teen-inch rainbow gobbled the hopper, I set, and both trout and I were hooked on tenkara.

Tenkara Dry Fly Gear

TENKARA DRY FLY RODS

You don't need to invest $1,000 in a rod, reel, and line to start fishing tenkara. Most tenkara rods sell for $89 to $250. I prefer Temple Fork Outfitter's "Dry Fly" model rod, an eleven-and-a-half-foot soft-action carbon fiber tenkara rod, for most of my dry fly fishing. The rod bends uniformly throughout, from butt to tip. I can easily load the rod and feel the loading of the line to allow a perfect forward cast without a tailing loop causing a tangle. This slow-action rod protects fine tippets and casts well into the wind. TFO's eight-and-a-half-foot rod, their "Cutthroat" model, works best for small streams and those waters with brushy banks and overhangs.

TENKARA DRY FLY LINES & LEADERS

Effective dry fly fishing with tenkara rods requires the use of one of two lines available to anglers on the market today. I prefer either a traditional furled or a fine-diameter level floating fly line. A furled line is one fashioned from several twisted, small-diameter fly-tying threads. Both work fine. I prefer furled lines from Zen Outfitters of Boise, Idaho, that are pretreated and float like a cork, or a ten- to fifteen-foot traditional level floating line. These lines require no babysitting to keep them floating on the surface.

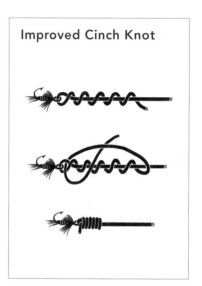

Improved Cinch Knot

Furled lines are very soft and supple and transmit the energy of the cast easily, making for efficient line and tippet turnover and great fly presentation. Furled lines come in various lengths. I prefer the thirteen-foot length. They easily attach to the rod end as they come with a hitching loop that you can hitch onto the braided lillian at the end of the rod. These also come with a stainless steel ring on the leader end, to which I add appropriate leader and tippets from 4X to 7X.

The other option, traditional level fly lines, are inexpensive and can be purchased complete in 80- to 100-foot lengths or bought in lengths cut from spools at most fly shops. I prefer a level line .021 inches in diameter, eight to fifteen feet long. Or better yet, cut both ends out of a DT000 line: one eight feet and the other fifteen feet in length. Both lines require tying a turle knot to loop over the lillian (see page 55). Leave a one-inch tag in the turle knot to loosen it in order to remove it from the lillian when not fishing. For the leader end of the line, you can tie a blood knot or surgeon's knot (see page 57) to make a standard seven-and-a-half-foot leader tapered to 3X or 4X and add tippets as needed.

KNOTS

Most anglers spend more time learning knots than they do learning to read the water or the insects that bring the trout to the surface. While knots are important to anglers, there are only a few that fly fishers must know. One secures the fly and the other ties on the tippet. A clinch or improved clinch knot is the easiest and best to learn for tying on the dry fly. The strongest for tippet-leader connections is the double surgeon's knot (see page 57).

SUNGLASSES & HATS

A hat with dark brim underside is a requirement for dry-fly sight fishing. I prefer one with a long bill that keeps the sun's rays from causing problems when searching into the sun for rising trout or tying to locate fish holding in the current. It also keeps snow and rain off my sunglasses.

Polarized sunglasses are important for all fishing situations. Not only do they protect your eyes from hooks, twigs, and branches when fishing, they cut the sun's glare and allow you to sight into the water and spot trout cruising and sipping insects on and under the surface. I prefer the "Igniter" glass lenses, a yellowish-gold color that serves dual purposes: on bright days these lenses cut the glare; they also brighten late evening light as it begins to fade, which brings on the best caddisfly emergences.

THE FISHING LIFE

Tenkara Can Save Money for More Fly Fishing Gear
Craig Mathews

Howard has come in every year early in the summer to buy the new, latest-and-greatest fly rods. Back then he was single, but about fifteen years ago he showed up with his new bride in tow. Sally stood at the counter, looking bored, gazing up at the framed mounted fly collections dotting the walls.

Over the next few years Howard and Sally added a couple of kids, Sarah and Emma. They too would come in staring at the fly tying materials and tee shirts with flies and fishing slogans on them. The girls also acted bored and couldn't wait to leave and head to their summer home in the valley to visit friends and their horses.

Last June, their first stop at the shop, they trudged in and again stared at the tee shirts and hats on the racks. Howard walked to the rod rack and began flexing a new $900 rod. I walked over to the tenkara rod rack and grabbed a $199 tenkara rod and began extending it while looking at the girls, smiling and reeling them in to check out the little tenkara rod.

As Howard asked me if the $900 rod was "what they all say it is," Emma asked me, "What kind of pole is that?" I'd extended it to its full length now as Howard replied for me, "Emma, that's one of those cane poles I used when I grew up catching brim in Alabama."

Emma, her mom, and sister Sarah were standing in front of me now, checking out the little tenkara rod, eyes wide open, listening to my stories of how simple and easy they were to fish. Sally turned and said to Howard, "Honey, I would learn to fly fish if I could have one of those." Emma and Sarah echoed Sally. A short while later out the door they hustled, Howard with his new $900 rod, the three ladies with one tenkara rod.

The following day Howard ran in the door of the shop and stumbled to the tenkara rod rack. I asked him, "How did your $900 rod work last night?" All he could say was, "Give me two more of those little cane poles—the girls out-fished me. I'll save a bundle not having to buy them $900 rods."

Now Sally and the girls are some of simple fly fishing's best ambassadors.

THE FISHING LIFE

The Gift

Craig Mathews

This last summer, I fished with my tenkara rod on the Firehole River in Yellowstone Park. I arrived as caddisflies were hatching and trout rose to them in the riffles and pools. I tied on an Iris Caddis emerger pattern and began taking a trout on almost every cast; with the tenkara, I could skip and dance my fly in each area where the trout were rising.

I heard a noise along the bank and turned to find several spectators lined up along the shore behind me. One young boy was at my hip, his mother apologizing, saying, "I'm sorry he got so close to you; he'd love to learn to fly fish." I replied, "Well, we'll take care of that right now." We walked a short distance to the next riffle with half the audience in tow. Within a few minutes, the lad had landed eight rainbows. I gave him the rod and he was on his way.

If you want to get a kid hooked on fishing, keep it simple—and make sure they quickly catch a fish.

Dry Fly Fishing with a Tenkara Rod

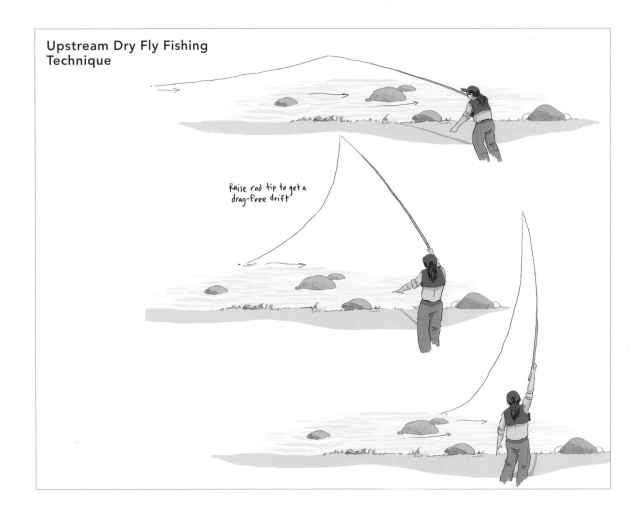

Upstream Dry Fly Fishing Technique

Raise rod tip to get a drag-free drift

As a rule, if you see fish rising, approach from downstream and work directly upstream. It is always best not to wade and to stay low to the bank so as not to present a silhouette that will spook the trout. If you must wade, by approaching from downstream you will not send debris and wading waves to the fish and signal your approach. Try to get within fifteen feet of the rising fish. Then present your fly about two feet upstream of the rising fish using a fixed-length, short-line, pinpoint-accurate cast (described below).

Allow the fly to approach the rising fish, and as the line begins to float back toward you, raise the rod by gradually bringing it up from a nine o'clock position to a twelve o'clock position, taking up the slack line as the line returns in the current. This allows the fly to float naturally and not be dragged by the downstream tension on the line from the current. It also keeps you in touch with your fly so when the fish does

Downstream Dry Fly Fishing Technique

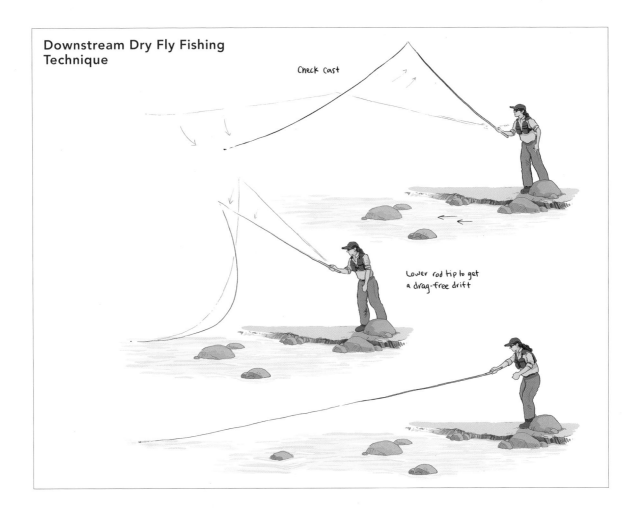

Check cast

Lower rod tip to get a drag-free drift

take the fly, you can set the hook and drive it home without having to take in slack line. If the fish does not take your offering, allow the fly to pass a foot or two beyond it and recast.

If searching water and fishing when no fish are rising, present your flies to all likely looking areas you expect trout to hold in with the same presentation as above. Wade slowly and carefully upstream, prospecting the water as you go.

There are times when a fish rises upstream or downstream of your position or near an obstruction like a weed bed, boulder, or mixed currents and prevents an upstream approach. In those cases, carefully wade from above or below to the rising fish. If wading from upstream, be careful not to send a wading wave or debris and spook the fish. Get as close to the fish as you can, preferably within twenty feet, and cast downstream, or upstream and across, with a slack-line accurate presentation. If wading downstream to the fish, mend once or twice as the fly drifts to the rising trout to delay drag and avoid a skittering/waking fly. The aim is to present the fly as naturally as possible.

Another effective presentation to use when trout rise downstream is to wade into position and cast bringing your rod-tip up to create enough slack line and use the tip of the rod to maneuver the fly to the fish, actually steering and guiding the fly into the fish's feeding lane. With a little practice you will do just fine, and catch far more trout with dry flies.

I prefer the upstream approach, but nothing is set in stone. Do whatever it takes to get close to a rising fish. Line drag is your enemy, and getting close to a rising fish helps to delay drag and stay in touch with your fly.

HOW TO MAKE A SHORT, SLACK, PINPOINT-ACCURATE CAST

The reason for using this cast is to delay drag on the fly. There are several ways to accomplish this cast, but my favorites are listed below. The two methods work with both tenkara and standard fly fishing gear.

With the first method, I choose the target, and if fishing standard rod and reel, I carry a bit of extra line in my line hand. If fishing tenkara, I let a short amount of slack line hang from the end of the rod. With tenkara, I never present a full-length line-and-leader cast that lands on a tight line, as this would usually result in immediate drag.

I guesstimate the spot I want my fly to land while accounting for current speed and drag. On my forward stroke, I aim for the spot where I want the fly to land. With tenkara, I make sure the extra line I cast allows enough slack to land on the water and give the fly time to drift naturally to the targeted fish. If fishing standard rod and reel and carrying extra line in my line hand, I stop the rod tip near the end of my forward stroke and at the same time release the extra slack line from my line hand, which allows the fly to reach my target with enough slack line to delay drag. This method will come naturally with a little experience.

With the second method, I follow the same two steps as with the first. On the third step, I aim for the spot; however, this time I follow through on the forward stroke and allow the fly to shoot beyond the target. As the line straightens, I stop my rod tip, causing the line to recoil and create slack line in a series of S-curves on the water. This method requires a feel and developed intuition, but with experience, it will become second nature.

Advanced Dry Fly Techniques

I usually fish one dry fly, but at times I knot on a second trailing dropper fly. Usually this occurs when I cannot determine what the fish are feeding on. During mayfly, caddis, or midge hatches, I might come upon several rising fish, and to quickly determine what stage of the insect the trout are feeding on, I tie on an emerger and a dun for instance.

To do this, leave a six- to eight-inch tag from your leader-tippet connection knot and tie one fly on here and the other on the end of your tippet. The distance between the leader-tippet connection knot to the point fly is eighteen to twenty-four inches.

Make sure the tag end is the heavier of the two pieces, as this helps keep the mono from tangling. Present the two flies, and using whichever pattern works best, remove the other fly and go with a one-fly presentation from there. Fishing two dry flies at the same time usually results in more tangles and hooks in the net mesh or your fingers when trying to release fish, but it is worth it when you are trying to find out what the fish are feeding on.

FALL: A SPECIAL TIME FOR ANGLERS

Fall is a favorite time for dry fly anglers. The summer crowds of fly fishers have left the rivers as big brown trout move upriver preparing to spawn. Other browns drop downstream from lakes into river and stream outlets, also preparing to spawn. Rainbow trout often follow browns on their spawning migrations. Most anglers targeting these big fall trout refer to them as runners. And, let's define this fall dry fly fishing as dry fly angling for fall migrating trout before their spawning begins. To fish for any trout actively spawning should not be attempted—trout must be allowed to spawn unmolested, as studies show wading through spawning beds can destroy most or all of the eggs.

Much has been written on effective presentation using big nymphs and streamers to take fall runners. Both these methods are effective, but there are dry fly methods that can produce even better during the right times.

Anglers should be alert to any insect emergence that brings trout to the surface to feed in fall. Tiny blue-winged olive mayflies emerge best on overcast, rainy or snowy afternoons, while midges emerge and bring big fall runners to the surface on both sunny and overcast days.

Many times I've come upon strong hatches of both insects and big trout rising to them in the quiet currents behind the spots other anglers are wading and pitching big weighted nymphs and streamers. By fishing dry flies I've often taken more fish and larger fish than those fishing big streamers and heavily weighted nymphs—simply by matching the fly to the small insects bringing the big runners to the surface to feed.

When fall runners become territorial before spawning, I do well fishing floating lines and unweighted flies like big #4-8 Nick's Sunken Stones. I fish the fly on a tight line across and downstream searching the seams and transition zones, swinging the fly on a tight line. It is exciting to watch a trout come several feet to the surface to take your floating fly.

On bright, sunny days when trout are not rising and reluctant to move far I'll fish a Simple Mouse, or frog, Nick's Stone, or a terrestrial pattern like a grasshopper, Black Foam Beetle, or cricket.

Remember this hint: When hooking or fighting a large trout using a tenkara rod there will be times you simply run out of line or can no longer run after a fish downstream. Don't hesitate to throw your rod in. I've thrown my rod more than a hundred times in order not to break the tippet and fish off. I have not lost a rod yet.

WINTER FISHING WITH TENKARA

The simple fly-fishing method using dry fly techniques for tenkara or traditional rod and reel is arguably the most effective and efficient for winter dry fly midge fishing. As we've said before, the tenkara rod has no guides or reel to freeze up in cold weather. It forces anglers to get close to rising fish to be able to keep track of one's fly. It allows anglers to better make short-line pinpoint-accurate casts that defeat line drag by keeping most fly line/leader off the water. Also due to colder winter water temps fish do not fight as hard, and that allows anglers to land trout quicker and easier than in summer.

The truth is most anglers are like I used to be. They might see midges on the water and not know they are being taken by rising trout. Wherever trout are found, so are midges. Most anglers overlook them, refusing to believe a trout would rise to such a tiny insect. Get over it: trout, big trout, love midges and our simple dry fly techniques work their magic taking big, rising trout on small midge fly patterns.

Because midges emerge year-round, anglers must be prepared to fish them at all times. If you see midges on the water, it is the strongest clue that trout are rising to them. But, from late fall into the spring season midges are often the only insect emerging and bringing trout to the surface to feed on them. So focus on fishing midge hatches during the winter months.

Audrey Herbert braves the cold with tenkara in hand on the Bow River, Canmore, Alberta. *Austin Trigg*

New Year's Day

Craig Mathews

It was New Year's Day, and the morning temperature broke the plus side of zero for the first time in two weeks. A herd of elk grazed below the house near the

Midges are an important source of food for trout during the winter months; their emergence and egg laying often take place at temperatures at or even below freezing. *John Juracek*

river. Since the cold had kept us inside for so long, we decided we would head to the river to see if we could catch our first trout of the New Year.

There was no wind, and the sun was blinding as it burned off the hoarfrost on grasses along the river. We put on our pac boots, grabbed our tenkara rods, and slogged through several inches of snow to the river.

Midges were already emerging along the shore, and clusters of mating midges the size of dimes were rolling through holding water behind boulders and in pockets and pools. We watched several nice trout rise casually to midge clusters and took turns catching a few rainbows before the sun's rays lost their punch and midge activity shut down for the day.

Dry Fly Fishing with a Rod and Reel

DRY FLY RODS

For rod-and-reel dry fly fishing, I like a slow, even-action rod. A slow rod forces me to slow down between casts and load the rod properly to recast, and to concentrate on my fly, the rises of fish, and the insects fish are feeding on. You need to get close to rising trout, and the slow action allows you to load the rod quickly with a short line and recast quickly too.

Slow-action rods also protect the fine tippets required in dry fly fishing by absorbing the shock of the trout taking the fly. My favorite traditional dry fly rod, while slow action, still has enough backbone to allow me to defeat heavy winds, pick line off the water, and present large bushy flies without false casting.

I like a simple single-action fly reel that is lightweight and has a click drag. There are many fine reels available that provide a good drag system and hold fifty yards of backing and can handle big, wild trout in heavy currents.

DRY FLY LINES, LEADERS, AND TIPPETS

The fly line is one of the foundations of successful dry fly fishing, yet few know much about it. Today's lines are made to last many days of use on rivers, lakes, and streams without babysitting. They need no maintenance except keeping them clean; they will float well and give many days of use.

Most weight-forward lines take up to 30 percent less space on reels than do double-tapered lines. And the same weight double-tapered and weight-forward lines have the same basic taper for the first thirty feet. Since nearly all my dry fly casting is done within thirty feet, I prefer the weight-forward line. With it I can put plenty of backing on my reel and make all my casts and presentations.

Even though there are hundreds of choices of leaders, it really is not that complicated. For dry fly fishing, I begin with a nine-foot knotless leader tapered down to 4X tippet.

Tie a three- to four-turn nail knot to connect the leader to the fly line using a simple nail knot tool. Add appropriate tippets of 5X, 6X, or 7X to the end of the leader depending on the fishing at hand.

If fishing a big salmonfly or grasshopper dry fly, cut the leader back a foot to 3X and knot the fly on there.

Skills and Guidelines for Dry Fly Fishing

Both expert and beginning fly fishers usually feel the most important ingredient to successful fly fishing is the right fly pattern. Yet the two most important things anglers—tenkara or rod and reel—must learn to be successful are proper presentation and technique. Too many anglers put their faith in realistic flies and long casts. And while some might agree proper presentation is the foundation of effective fly fishing, few actually practice the basics.

One day on a favorite spring creek where big trout are hard to approach and catch, I watched an old man creep along at a snail's pace, never wading but using streamside cover to get within fifteen to twenty feet of rising trout. He used a short, soft, pinpoint, slack-line cast to defeat drag and took several big fish. That same day, I watched another angler who advocates powerful rods and long presentations bang out sixty- to eighty-foot casts and spook every trout he fished to. He failed to take even one trout that day.

Here are a few tips on approaching the river during a hatch or covering water when there are no insects bringing fish to the surface.

• If you want to fish dry flies during an insect emergence, be on the water when they are expected. Check weather forecasts as well as wind and water conditions.

• Observe other anglers, if present, to see what direction they are heading to avoid crowding.

• Observe the conditions. Is there insect activity like caddis or mayfly, terrestrials or midges? If there are no insects or rises, pick a dry fly that imitates an insect trout will recognize as food.

• Recognize the different riseforms trout make when taking mayflies, caddisflies, terrestrial insects, damsel and dragonflies, or midges.

• When trout are rising all around, it is very difficult to take the time to find the seine and check for clues as to what the trout are rising to. Do it anyway. The seine will show you what the trout are feeding on—the river will tell you what to do.

• Longer casts result in bad presentation, and you lose track of the fly. It is always best to be patient and hold your fire rather than present a long cast and spook the fish.

Peter Kullman prospects for shy trout, Saxån River, Sweden. *Gösta Fries*

• Never jump in wading and spraying your casts. Wade as little as possible, and keep a low profile. Wading spooks small fish upstream where they might alert larger trout. Wading also destroys trout spawning nests, upsets trout habitat, and kills aquatic insects.

• Get as close to rising trout as possible. You can get very close to trout from downstream, and it will help you keep from casting into and across mixed currents to defeat drag. Usually I scooch or slide along the shoreline on my butt or walk on my knees on the shore or in the water to get within fifteen to twenty feet of rising trout. Waders with built-in kneepads are a necessary part of my equipment for getting close to trout.

• Count the trout's rise rhythm, and if, for instance, the trout is feeding every four seconds, put your fly in front of it in four seconds, and if on still water, cast in front of the fish the same distance as between its past rises.

• If coming from upstream, don't send a wading wave or debris that would put the rising fish down, maybe for the day.

• If there are several trout rising, pick one and concentrate on presenting an accurate cast to it. Don't spray casts among rising fish; that will certainly spook them.

Hilary Oliver catches and releases her first fish ever on the Fall River, Idaho. Is this fishing fun or what? *Jeremy Koreski*

• Use a short, slack, pinpoint-accurate cast, as fish work in very narrow feeding lanes and will not move far for a natural or for your fly. Do not false cast over the fish, as they will see the line or be spooked by water drops.

• Watch your fly closely as it approaches the rising fish. Often, you will see the fish fin up and inspect your offering and then turn away.

• If that is the case, it is important to rest the trout for a minute to allow it a confidence rise or two before presenting the fly again while paying greater attention to the drift of the fly. Drag must be avoided; it is usually the reason the fish didn't take the fly on the first cast.

• When trout are rising and the evening light is getting low and making it tough to see your fly, use a short cast and adjust your position in relation to the trout so you can keep track of your fly and rises to it.

• Dead drifting, twitching, high floating, and pulling a dry fly under the surface should all be tried and will, at times, entice some trout when all else fails.

• Wear earth-toned clothing to prevent unnatural contrast with natural surroundings.

• Do not give up. Trout may be sleeping. Yes, they do. If there is no hatch and every fly you try fails to bring fish up, take a break and return later.

• Present the fly two feet above the rising trout, allowing it to float drag-free to the fish. If the fly is not taken, let it float by the fish two feet before carefully lifting it off the water to recast. Do not allow it to float further or it may become snagged or wrapped around a rock, and getting it free will usually alert the trout or spook it away.

• Learn to spot trout whether they are aggressively rising or barely dimpling the surface of the water to take an insect. This takes a little patience, practice, and good sunglasses. Too, the best anglers learn to see trout moving under the surface taking nymphs and emergers. It does not take long to see a fish's shadow against the bottom as it holds or moves, or the trout's white mouth as it opens to take a nymph subsurface. Once you learn to see and spot fish, you can present your fly to them and increase your overall catch rate.

• Use boulders, logs, and logjams to cover your approach. I also use these obstructions to cast over and to drape my line over to absorb drag when presenting a fly to trout—they keep fly line and leaders off the water where they are subject to current drag.

• When fishing from a drift boat, position the boat so that you are within twenty to thirty feet of the bank and your target. Since the boat is traveling at the same speed as your fly you will have a long, drag-free drift without the need to recast or mend. Using a fixed length cast enables you to keep the boat at the same distance from shore, allowing your fly to be in front of rising fish or in the best holding water for most of the float. You can also anchor the boat so you can fish from a stationary boat.

• When floating, be courteous to wading anglers. If you are rowing, give wading fishermen plenty of room. Drift by as far away from them as possible; don't bump the oars in the boat or the boat on the bottom of the river.

• I find myself fishing dry flies more and more as living creatures, trying to imitate how they would react when exposed to water and trout. Whether fishing an egg-laying caddis, emerging midge pattern skittering on the surface film to escape its pupal shuck, or grasshoppers blown into the water by heavy winds kicking frantically back to shore—try to envision the scenario you are trying to recreate. Experiment imparting different motions to flies. Skitter and wake caddis patterns on the surface by raising your rod and twitching the line, or moving the rod tip side to side. Cast a frog or mouse fly along the shoreline and move by jerking it in four- to eight-inch quick strips. Try moving your fly to imitate what a natural insect, frog, or mouse would do, and then hang on because the fish's take is usually vicious!

THE FISHING LIFE

The Pope Isn't Always Right
Craig Mathews

Pope is West Yellowstone's longest active guide. Now in his midseventies, he still runs with the rookie guides, but his knowledge of fishing and Yellowstone country unique techniques and strategies is unmatched.

When tenkara first came on the scene a few years back Pope announced, "You'll never get me using one of those bamboo poles." He added, "My folks mostly want to float, and I can just imagine the disaster hooking a big trout with only twenty feet of line while floating along at three to four miles per hour would create."

A couple of Pope's favorite clients, Amy and Steve, arrived at the shop an hour before they were to meet Pope for a float trip early last July. Amy, much to Steve's chagrin, asked about purchasing a tenkara rod to fish on their float that day. I tried to explain that Pope might not allow her to fish the rod or even bring it along in the boat that day. Amy simply stated, "Leave it up to me; he will let me try it."

Amy stowed the rod in her gear bag and the three left an hour later for the Madison River.

About 4:00 p.m. that afternoon, Pope ran through the front door and yelled to me, "Give me two of those poles—I've never had more fun fishing than today."

It turned out Amy had landed several fine trout with the tenkara, and Pope learned some new fishing techniques to teach along with earning a nice steak dinner that night and a healthy tip from Amy and Steve!

The Young Leading the Old

Craig Mathews

Last summer I taught two very experienced spring creek anglers how to fish tenkara, but they struggled for an hour before picking it up. Both were typical of experienced anglers learning a new method. The men were quite honestly insecure, lacked confidence, and tended to overthink the simple and easy processes of tenkara. What turned the tide was when a six-year-old nephew of one of the men took my rod and began catching small trout on a grasshopper dry fly within minutes, much to the men's chagrin. Soon they both learned the proper dry fly tenkara technique from the six-year-old.

Guides—Yvon Chouinard, Millie Paini, Anne Marie Emery, and Mark Harbaugh—with some happy kids after a day of tenkara class on the Henry's Fork, Idaho. *Bryan Gregson*

Useful Dry Fly Patterns

While there are thousands of effective dry fly patterns for fishing the varous hatches and insects, the ones I list here are simple to tie and proven to catch big trout. This short list should prepare the anglers for the entire year of dry fly fishing.

MAYFLY DUNS AND SPINNERS

We developed the Sparkle Dun pattern to imitate most emerging mayfly species. This fly in a few different sizes and colors will fill 95 percent of your mayfly fishing needs.

YELLOW-TAN AND OLIVE SPARKLE DUNS

Note: All Sparkle Duns are tied in the same style; the differences are in size and body color to match natural insects.

Hook:	#12 to #20, dry fly
Thread:	8/0 gray is a good neutral color for all Sparkle Dun types
Tail (shuck):	Mayfly brown Zelon one-half to a full hook shank in length
Body:	To match naturals, yellow-tan and olive are most common
Wing:	Natural deer hair

RUSTY AND OLIVE SPARKLE SPINNERS

Hook:	#12 to #20, dry fly
Thread:	8/0 gray
Tail:	Dun or cream hackle fibers
Body:	To match naturals, with rusty and olive the most common
Wing:	White Zelon tied spent, half spent, or upright

BLUE-WINGED OLIVES AND MAHOGANY SOFT-HACKLE DUNS/SPINNERS

Tied as a dun, by trimming off bottom hackle this fly can be fished as an effective imitation of a mayfly spinner.

Note: All soft-hackle duns and spinners are tied in the same style; the differences are in size and body color to match natural insects.

Hook:	#12-22, dry fly
Thread:	8/0 rusty dun
Tail:	Lemon wood duck flank fibers
Body:	Dubbing to match naturals: olive, yellow, mahogany
Wing & legs:	Hungarian partridge mixed with dun or grizzly

GREEN DRAKE AND GRAY DRAKE FOAM SPINNERS

Casting a large size #10-14 spinner imitation is a recipe for wind knots. Using hackle to imitate the wings on large spinner patterns minimizes this and maintains a nice spinner profile. Adding closed-cell foam over the wing aids in the floatation of this important large fly pattern.

Hook:	#10-14 dry fly
Thread:	8/0 rusty dun
Tail:	Grizzly hackle fibers
Body:	To match naturals: olive, gray, and tan most common
Rib:	Brown thread for gray and brown drakes, yellow for green drakes
Wing case:	Gray closed-cell foam
Wing:	4-5 wraps of grizzly saddle hackle trimmed top and bottom

AMBER AND OLIVE IRIS CADDIS

Note: All Iris Caddis are tied in the same style; the differences are in size and body color to match natural insects.

Hook:	#14 to #18, dry fly
Thread:	8/0 gray
Shuck:	Amber Zelon
Body:	Amber, tan, or olive Zelon dubbing blend
Wing:	Dun or white Zelon looped and tied low over body
Head:	Hare's mask shaggy

X2 CADDIS IN TAN AND OLIVE

Hook:	#14 to #18, dry fly
Thread:	8/0 gray
Shuck:	Amber Zelon
Body:	Zelon dubbing blend of olive or tan
Rib:	One strand of pearl Krystal Flash wrapped five times up the body
Wing:	Natural deer hair

CDC EGG-LAYING CADDIS

Note: All egg-laying caddis are tied in the same style; the differences are in size and color to match naturals.

Hook:	#14-18 dry fly
Thread:	8/0 rusty dun
Egg sac:	Insect green Zelon fibers
Abdomen:	CDC dubbing
Wing:	CDC fibers
Head/thorax:	Hare's Ear dubbing

NICK'S GIANT AND GOLDEN SUNKEN STONES

Hook:	#6 to #10, dry fly
Thread:	6/0 to match body color
Tail/egg sac:	Black poly yarn
Body:	Orange Zelon dubbing for giant stone, yellow for golden stone
Wing:	Five to seven clumps of deer hair

LITTLE YELLOW STONE ADULT

Hook:	#12 to #16, dry fly
Thread:	8/0 yellow
Tag:	Red Zelon
Body:	Little yellow stonefly Zelon dubbing blend
Wing:	Yellow dyed elk or deer hair
Hackle:	Grizzly or ginger

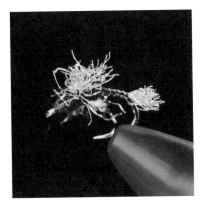  

ZELON MIDGE

Hook:	#20 and #22, dry fly
Thread:	8/0 gray
Shuck:	Dun Zelon
Body:	Thread wrapped over Zelon Shuck
Thorax:	Midge black Zelon dubbing blend
Wing:	Dun Zelon
Head:	Black Zelon dubbing blend

GRIFFITH'S GNAT

Hook:	#16 to #20, dry fly
Thread:	8/0 gray
Body:	Two to three strands of peacock herl
Hackle:	Grizzly palmered through body, four to six wraps

SCOTTY'S MIDGE

This important fly can be tied by anyone, beginner and expert alike. It imitates a skittering midge trapped in its pupal shuck.

Hook:	#18-24 dry fly
Thread:	8/0 rusty dun
Shuck:	Coachman red Zelon fibers
Abdomen:	Wraps of thread over shuck
Thorax:	Black dubbing
Wing:	Deer hair

BLUE AND OLIVE FOAM DAMSELS

Hook:	#10, dry fly
Thread:	8/0 gray
Body:	Strip cut of closed-cell foam (or braided mono) in blue or olive
Wing:	Clear or white Medallion sheeting cut to shape, or white Zelon tied spent
Hackle:	Wraps of grizzly hackle in front of wings

BLUE AND RED FOAM DRAGONS

Hook:	#10, dry fly
Thread:	8/0 gray
Body:	Thick strip cut of closed-cell foam (or braided mono) in blue or red
Wing:	Clear or white Medallion sheeting cut to shape, or white Zelon tied spent

CINNAMON AND BLACK ZELON FLYING ANTS

Hook:	#14 and #16, dry fly
Thread:	8/0 black
Body:	Closed-cell foam, black or cinnamon
Wing:	White Zelon
Legs:	Fine black rubber legs

FOAM BEE

Hook:	#14, dry fly
Thread:	8/0 black
Body:	Striped black and yellow foam body material
Wing:	White Zelon
Hackle:	Grizzly

BLACK FOAM BEETLE

Hook:	#14 and #16, dry fly
Thread:	8/0 black
Body:	Black dubbing, or omit
Shell (back):	Black closed-cell foam strip pulled over body
Legs:	Black round rubber legs
Indicator:	Orange closed-cell foam
Head:	Butt of foam used for shell back

CHAOS GRASSHOPPER

Hook:	#12 and #14, dry fly
Thread:	6/0 brown
Body:	Tan closed-cell foam
Legs:	Yellow rubber legs and brown hackle (optional)
Indicator:	Orange closed-cell foam
Wing:	Pale yellow Zelon

BLACK FOAM CRICKET

Hook:	#10, dry fly
Thread:	6/0 black
Body:	Black closed-cell foam
Legs:	Black rubber legs
Indicator:	Bright orange yarn, or omit

SPRUCE MOTH

Hook:	#12, dry fly
Thread:	8/0 rusty dun
Body:	Amber Zelon dubbing blend
Wing:	Deer hair

ADAMS CRIPPLE

Hook:	#16, dry fly
Thread:	8/0 gray
Tail/Shuck:	Mayfly brown Zelon
Body:	Fine gray dubbing
Wing:	White Zelon
Hackle:	Mixture of wraps of brown and grizzly

ROYAL WULFF CRIPPLE

Hook:	#14, dry fly
Thread:	8/0 black
Tail/Shuck:	Mayfly brown Zelon
Body:	Peacock herl and red floss
Wing:	White Zelon
Hackle:	Brown

SIMPLE FROG AND EASY MOUSE

These flies were developed to imitate frogs and mice found on rivers, ponds, lakes, and streams around the world. Trout like protein and these flies fit that bill for big trout everywhere!

Hook:	#2-6 dry fly or stinger hook
Thread:	6/0 olive or rusty dun
Leg:	Splayed green dyed grizzly neck hackle
Flash:	Crystal flash fibers (optional)
Body:	Green preformed foam body
Eyes:	Glued on body (optional)

Hook:	#4-6 long shank dry fly
Thread:	6/0 rusty dun
Tail:	Ultra chenille tan or dark gray
Body:	Brown and grizzly mixed and trimmed off bottom
Head:	Trimmed tan or gray closed-cell or furry foam
Eyes:	Trimmed piece of gray or black foam (optional)
Whiskers:	Hackle fibers left untrimmed after winding body hackle

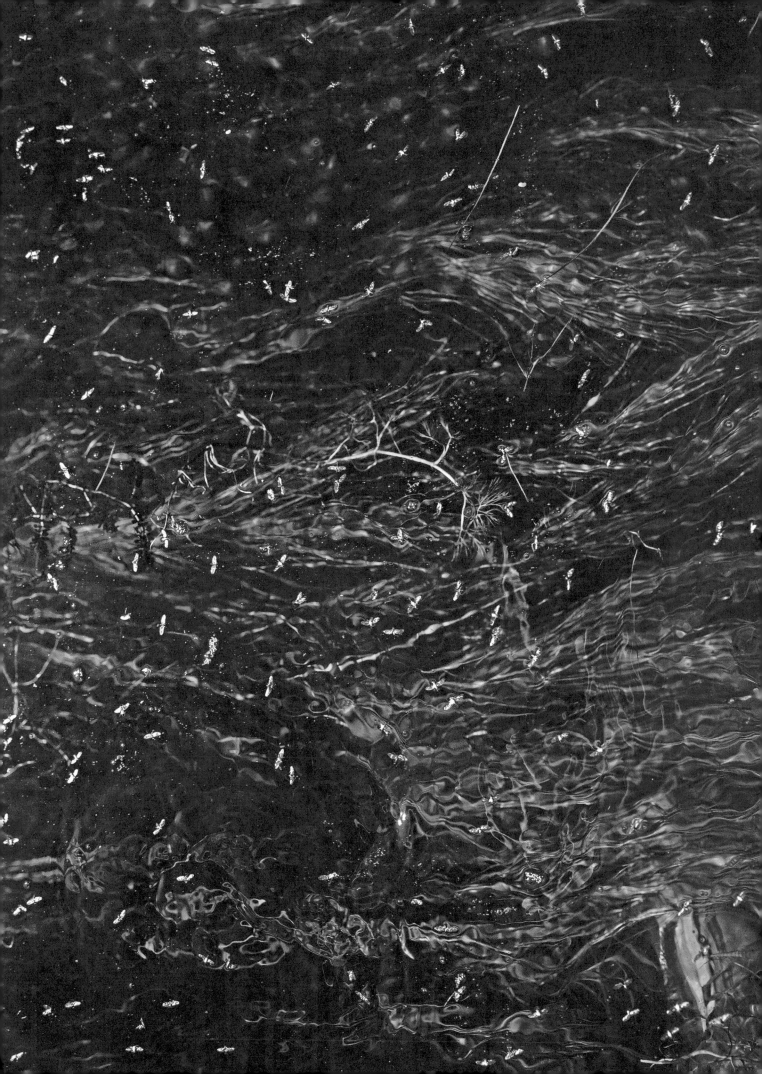

CHAPTER 5
Fishing Situations
YVON CHOUINARD, CRAIG MATHEWS, & MAURO MAZZO

Fishers who declare that they fish only with dry flies, or nymphs, or streamers, or cast only to rising fish, regardless of the conditions, will often find themselves fishing in an ineffective way.

Certain rivers, or parts of rivers, can be fished most effectively with very specific techniques. When you add the season of the year, the time and conditions of the day, the insect activity at that hour, and so on, you have a puzzle that cannot be solved with a single technique.

However, there is no need for the average angler to be an entomologist. You need not know the difference between a mahogany dun nymph and a pale morning dun nymph. You can even forget about emergence dates, fly sex, maturity, and immaturity. You need not always have to match the hatch. Look at the water in front of you, break it down into segments, and think about where the fish are holding and where you need to be to present a fly to them: develop a simple, effective plan.

OPPOSITE: A trico spinner fall on the Henry's Fork spring creek, Idaho. Can you spot the fly? Just kidding. *Jeremy Koreski*

PREVIOUS SPREAD: Turbulent water, to be sure, but plenty of trout live along the quiet edges of the Lamar River, Wyoming. This is ideal water for a heavy nymph. *John Juracek*

The Innovator
Yvon Chouinard

I clearly remember the most memorable trout that I've ever caught. I had spotted a large Snake River cutthroat sipping pale morning duns (PMDs) on Flat Creek in Jackson Hole. I've found that cutthroats feeding on PMDs can be extremely selective, often keying in on only one stage of the mayfly.

This fish was feeding close to the cutbank of this meadow creek just below a little snag. It would take a delicate curve cast to the left to avoid the snag, and the best I could get would be a two-foot-long drift.

After countless tries, I finally started to get the cast down, but the clever fish had no interest in my dry fly. I cast and rested the fish and cast again for almost an hour. Finally, I put it all together with a combination of 7X tippet, a lucky curve cast, and a stripped-down size 20 PMD dry fly that I converted into a "physically challenged emerger." The final solution was to put spittle on the back third of the fly so it hung below the surface film. Don't be afraid to experiment; try different things, and figure out what works.

ABOVE: A pheasant-tail soft hackle fooled this Yellowstone cutthroat, Montana. *Emily Gribble*

BELOW: A bull trout swims near it's redd, Cultus Creek, British Columbia. *Bruce Kirkby*

OPPOSITE: Craig Mathews reads the rocks. Madison River, Montana. *Patrick Daigle*

The Fish
Mauro Mazzo

When I start fishing, I try to think like a fish or at least try to guess where a fish would stay and what it is going to do. I look around for likely places, like boul-

ders, that offer good cover and a continual supply of food. For instance, you might think that the middle of a big pool in a sizeable river is the best place, but most of the time it is the worst; the middle of the pool is where the fish are more exposed to predators. You will find only small fish there, and we want to catch the big one.

The first places you want to look at are nice rocks at the tails of pools. Those are the first places I would stay if I were a fish. Going upstream, if I were a fish, I would hang under the edges of the current that is created by big boulders. On those edges a fish would certainly have larvae or insects drifting down with the current.

The best places for fish are ones that have plenty of cover. Nice big-pocket water is the best place for the big fish to be and where they can find easy food. It's like having a holiday in Mexico: you lie down, wait for the food, and then go back to your beach chair. That's what fish want to do; fish are lazy.

THE FISHING LIFE

The Detective
Craig Mathews

Angling legend Charlie Brooks once said, "The single most important thing a fly fisher can know is the character and quality of the rivers and streams he or she fishes."

Three things often limit the success of anglers, beginners and experienced alike: trying to fish too much water in too little time, a lack of simple planning, and using inappropriate tools, methods, or techniques. Knowing what to expect on the rivers, lakes, and streams you plan to fish can save you time and money and result in huge successes. There is much fly fishing information available online, in books, at local fly shops, and from fly fishing guides and clubs. Armed with this information, anglers can be prepared to fish their target waters in most fishing situations.

Before you can catch fish, you have to know where the fish are and what they are eating. You have to do a little homework. You have to know what to expect and have an initial concept of when to switch from nymph to wet or to dry. Read books, research online, talk to those who know; find out what bugs to expect and the dates of emergence for those bugs for your target river. Bring a little net to find out what bugs are on the river when you get there. Look under rocks, around bushes, and in the air. Do what the river tells you to do.

Fast Mountain Waters

Rivers and streams that flow through canyons or gorges are usually rough-and-tumble waters. Most are rich in insect life. They tumble over boulders and jagged rocks and are hard or impossible to wade—and sometimes dangerous. Wade rough-and-tumble waters as little as possible to avoid a dunking.

In rough-and-tumble waters, trout need relief from heavy currents. Most first-timers focus on the standing waves of white water as they crash around huge boulders and snags of timber. But anglers should disregard the rough water in the middle of the river and instead concentrate on the slower margins—the pockets and pools along the edges. Fish the river as you would a small trout stream.

Trout do not occupy every inch of a fast, rough stream or river. And they will not move far for a natural or artificial fly. It is important to fish only the holding water where fish are lying and accustomed to getting their groceries. Holding water also gives trout protection and security.

This type of water is the easiest to read and learn because of all the clues it offers: visible currents, foam lines, pockets, pools, seams, and obstructions like boulders and logjams. An added plus is the noise of the waves and heavy currents that allows fishers to get close to holding water without spooking fish.

Visible currents are created as water moves swiftly around boulders and waterfalls or as it whirlpools and bubbles behind downed timber. These currents are easy to see, and relief from them means big trout will be present—and usually lots of them.

Foam lines are apparent but are seldom recognized as the conveyer belt bringing food to, or providing escape routes for, trout. Thin foam lines appear behind or next to boulders in the main current or along boulders next to the bank where several currents may merge. Below this, the foam line spreads out, and at this point, in the broader and slower currents, trout begin to hold and feed. The foam lines must be six inches or wider before trout will use them for cover, feeding, and relief from heavy currents.

A pocket is deep water located below a logjam or boulder. Fish use pockets like they use foam lines.

Seams are the transition water most trout prefer to hold in. The water separating the quiet water on the inside from the fast water on the outside of boulders is a good example. There are seams on and beneath the surface. They may be associated with visible currents, pockets, undercuts, foam lines, or logjams. As anglers put in more time on the water, they will come to readily recognize more productive seams. Seams can be counted on to produce more good trout than any other area.

WET FLY FISHING FAST MOUNTAIN WATERS

Fast mountain streams are caddis and stonefly water; I wouldn't bother with small flies. This is good water to do the two-fly, soft-hackle and dry caddis technique. Use a large attractor soft hackle like a size 8 or 10 for the point fly and a large buoyant dry fly for the dropper.

Cast downstream so the point fly enters first into every piece of soft water, foam line, eddy, or pocket. Sometimes in rough water you can bounce the dropper fly off the top of little waves. If that doesn't result in a strike, drag the soft hackle upstream and into the same areas.

You can also run a streamer through these same places. If there is a suck hole or reversal, drop the streamer in it and the fly will get sucked down so you can get the fly down deeper into the next pocket.

– *Yvon Chouinard*

Jeremiah Watt negotiates the rough-and-tumble water of Big Cottonwood Creek, Utah. *Jay Beyer*

The Plan River is a very secluded place with almost no fishing pressure. Alto Adige, Italy. *Mauro Mazzo*

NYMPH FISHING FAST MOUNTAIN WATERS

Keep the casting to a minimum in this kind of water to avoid spooking fish. In very small pockets, do not cast at all, and just drop the fly right above the spot you want to fish.

The easiest way to fish the nymph in this kind of water is to use a tandem formed by a big dry fly and a lightly weighted nymph tied under the dry at a distance of about one and a half times the average depth of that stretch of water. The use of a speed dropper like the one Yvon describes in the wet fly tenkara section (see page 66) will give you the opportunity to remove it quickly and switch back to fishing with only the one nymph when you find a deeper pool so you can fish it properly.

You will see some spots on a steep creek that look impossible to fish but often hold some big fish. The most common spot is the area under an overhanging tree with branches touching the water. An impossible place to cast to, but there is a solution—a dirty trick.

Walk upstream of the spot—preferably on the riverbank, not in the water—making the least noise possible. Position yourself about twenty-five feet upstream of the spot. Tie a big caddis on the dropper, and use a small weighted nymph as the point fly. Put the fly on the water, and shaking the rod tip, let out enough line so your rig gets under the branches. If there is a fish around, he will take it.

– *Mauro Mazzo*

DRY FLY FISHING FAST MOUNTAIN WATERS

When fishing dry flies, you want to be fishing rough-and-tumble waters when insect activity occurs. If you want to fish a caddis hatch, you should arrive late in the day as caddis emergences occur in the evenings. This is where planning for success is so important.

Slowly walk the banks and fish every hold, pocket, and seam. If you suspect trout will be rising to an expected hatch, walk well back from the banks to avoid disturbing the water.

If there is an emergence of caddis or mayflies, match it and fish accordingly. If no fish are rising and no insects are active, pick a fly that imitates an insect trout recognize as food for that time period.

On rough water, trout often appear to be rising to mayfly duns riding the surface. Pick a fish and present your cast while observing the fish. If the trout lets duns pass as it continues to rise in the holding water, switch to an emerger or wingless floating fly or cut the wing off the dry fly you are using.

If fishing midges, anglers should keep in mind that trout working midges in rough-and-tumble conditions do so in thin water. They are very hard to approach and usually you will get only one drift over them. These fish are used to deep water with cover, heavy flows, and security, so try not to wade when getting close enough to present a cast.

The finest dry fly angling on rough-and-tumble waters occurs when female salmonflies return to the water to lay eggs during the afternoon. It is important to locate the area on the river when and where the females are laying their eggs to be successful.

Never be without a mouse or frog fly pattern when fishing fast mountain waters. Both species occupy the streamside vegetated areas along the rough-and-tumble waters and can fall, hop, or run into them at times. Big trout patrol the shoreline searching for insects and protein-rich mice and frogs. Fish the frog or mouse as a living creature, hopping it off the shore, skittering it along the bank, or having it fall from overhanging sticks, logs, or vegetation into the water. I'll never forget watching a young angler net a fifteen-inch rainbow he took on a Simple Frog fly pattern on the Gallatin River in southwest Montana last summer. Sliding the fish into the net as I approached from downstream, he looked back with a big smile on his face. Just then the fish, resting in the net bag, regurgitated a fat chipmunk it had previously eaten.

– Craig Mathews

Old School

Mauro Mazzo

The old ways die hard: Arturo Pugno, 'the Valsesiana master,' fishing with his sixty-year-old solid cane rod on the Sesia River, Italy. He spotted a good grayling in the fast current. *Mauro Mazzo*

One of the Valsesia's old fishing masters, Arturo Pugno, told me about a style of fishing where they tied a special rig made with three hooks and a dead fish on one of the hooks. Then they maneuvered it into the broken water under a cascade to give the marble trout the illusion of a wounded fish.

They were fishing with no reel, using heavy cane rods with a rope attached to the butt. When they hooked a fish that was really big, they threw the rod in the water and watched it until it got close to the bank, a sign that the fish was tired. If that didn't happen, they had to jump in the water and swim after it.

Arturo's biggest marble trout was more than fifteen pounds. After more than an hour, the fish was not coming close to the bank, and he decided to swim in the river, grab the rod, and pull the fish in. This was nothing unusual for him, except that it was February and the temperature was many degrees below freezing.

That Old Guy

Craig Mathews

Last summer, I watched four anglers fishing an area the size of a pool table for two hours on a rough-and-tumble water stretch of the Madison River. As I sat on the opposite side of the river fishing a caddis emergence, catching and releasing several trout, I noted they were not taking a single fish. I knew why. The water they presented their flies in was six inches deep and very swift, not the water trout would hold or feed in. Still, the anglers cast and cast and switched positions several times.

The next day, I saw their vehicle as it pulled up in front of our shop. The four young anglers strolled into the store, and I asked how their fishing had been. They said they'd just pulled in late yesterday from a marathon drive all the way from Atlanta, Geor-

The "old guy" at his tying desk, Blue Ribbon Flies, West Yellowstone, Montana. *Patrick Daigle*

gia, and had fished the night before but had not taken a fish. They said something about an old guy across the river from them taking fish last night. I could not resist and told them "that old guy was me." I gave the red-faced newbies a few Iris Caddis emergers and drew them a map of where to expect rising fish near the Three Dollar Bridge along the Madison.

The next morning, they came in with fresh coffee and a donut for "the old guy," thanking me for showing them where to fish during evening caddis on rough water like the Madison River.

THE FISHING LIFE

Locals Only

Craig Mathews

I will never forget locating the secret "locals" pond in Yellowstone with Labrador-sized brook trout. I was still police chief in West Yellowstone, and Larry, the town's attorney, had hinted its location to me that summer. When cop matters

quieted in September, my wife, Jackie, and I headed out one frosty fall morning to find the pond he told me about that reportedly held four- to five-pound brook trout. We'd sloshed a couple of miles through beaver-dammed backwaters along a smooth-flowing stream where the tiny pond was hinted to be. Resting at a small spring inlet pond dammed by beavers, I told Jackie we had gone far enough and had to go back to Larry for more clues. Just then, three huge brook trout, as if on cue, jumped simultaneously not ten feet in front of us. It turned out we didn't need to go back to Larry; we had found the pond after all.

The shallow, still waters of a beaver pond require a stealthy approach, long delicate leaders, and a "soft" presentation. Idaho. *John Juracek*

Slow Meadow Waters

This water type is typically a meandering meadow stream with even, smooth currents interspersed with riffles and pools. Reading this water requires lots of bank walking, concentration, great eyesight, and plenty of patience, but it also may provide a few pleasant surprises like huge trout rising to the surface that leave barely a dimple.

Beginning anglers should also be on the watch for fish migration on slow meadow waters. An area that fishes well one day may be devoid of trout the next. Some feel that fish do not adopt a permanent holding spot on slow meadow waters. On many smooth rivers and streams, it pays to move and cover lots of water if you fail to raise fish in spots where you had recently found them.

Sound and vibrations transmit very far on these meadow creeks. You need to walk very quietly to avoid spooking these fish. You really should be barefooted or wearing leather moccasins.

There are four features found on slow meadow waters that concentrate insects and trout rising to them. You should watch for whirlpools, back currents, scum lines, and feeding troughs.

Whirlpools are formed when currents work around logs, sweepers, and islands. Look for back currents that collect insects at the end of whirlpools. Be alert here for single trout, and whole pods, that will come to the surface for terrestrial imitations like ants, bees, grasshoppers, and crickets as well as insect emergences of mayflies and caddis. Due to the direction of flow in whirlpools and back currents, trout may face downstream.

Scum lines and feeding troughs are found where currents come together. Slow meadow waters hold areas where one current sweeps along an overhanging bank as another current comes off a weed bed or obstruction like a log and merges with it at a gravel ledge. These scum lines provide tight feeding lanes, and trout will seldom move far to take a fly. In places like this, trout might drop back to where two scum lines come together to form a longer, wider lane known as a feeding trough. The troughs might be several feet wide and several feet long and hold dozens of trout.

Other excellent places are the potential shelters close to the bank. Undercut banks and logs and stones breaking the current along the bank create ideal habitat for fish. Also search the pocket water created by a stone or a log breaking the water's flow midstream. The fish will often hold in this calm water, feeding on the two currents in which the main current has been split by the obstruction. Check also for any deeper and slower stretches.

The long evenings of June provide plenty of time for fishing on the Madison River in Yellowstone Park. *John Juracek*

WET FLY FISHING SLOW MEADOW WATERS

Soft hackles will work whenever there is a bit of depth (more than six inches) and moving water. You will catch mostly small fish in the shallow water except in the early mornings or evenings, when there can be some larger fish.

Inside every bend of the stream, there will be a deep pool. That's where the big fish are, tucked down deep under the undercut banks. They don't like to come out for anything small or that isn't at their depth. In the evenings, fish with heavy streamers to draw out these big brown or brook trout.

– *Yvon Chouinard*

On a meadow or spring creek, the larger fish are holed up under the undercut banks. South Fork of the Madison, Montana. *John Juracek*

NYMPH FISHING SLOW MEADOW WATERS

The prime waters for the nymph fishers here are the undercut banks and the deeper waters.

Undercut banks are some of the most interesting water on a small stream; these are the places where the big guys hide. Here, your chances of success depend on the way you approach the stream. The noise made by your walking will scare the fish, so you have to move either like a ballet dancer or a special-forces member. They are quite different people, but both of them are really good at moving lightly; choose the style that suits your personality.

You will need to fish either at short or medium distance. If you are able to see the nymph in the water, short-distance sight fishing will be your choice. Cast as close to the bank as possible and follow the drift of your fly with your eyes. If you see anything happening close to your fly, like a sudden flash or a shadow covering the fly, strike. Often, that flash or shadow is a fish. If you have a problem seeing the fly or if the water is colored, use an indicator made with a piece of fluorescent nylon, or use a dry fly as an indicator.

There are strike indicators that look like a small float that you can buy in a fly fishing shop, but consider that the bigger the indicator, the more takes you will miss. This happens for two reasons. Very often, the fish takes the fly and spits it back out very quickly because it realizes there is something wrong; in this case, you will not even see the smallest movement in the float. The second reason is connected to this first. The resistance offered from the strike indicator to the nymph affects its drift and will increase the chances that the fish realizes there is something wrong and refuses your fly completely.

It is better yet to use a dry fly as an indicator. Working a nymph suspended to a dry fly will make it much more effective to fish the undercut banks: the fly will pass in front of the nose of the fish at the fish's depth, and you will be able to fish at longer distances, thereby reducing the chances of spooking the fish. Cast as close to the bank as possible and follow the drift of your fly with your eyes. If you see your indicator stop, strike immediately.

As a general rule, remember that we are trying to make a fish believe that a bunch of hair, fur, and feathers is real food. We should feel obliged to present it with the most natural drift. Otherwise we would be shameless.

If you are fishing a pool, the first place to look will be its head, where the food taken by the current settles down. Normally, there are also fish at the tails of the pools, but because the water is often shallower there, it is a better spot for the wet or dry fly fisher.

More often than not, it is mandatory to fish upstream, so the most effective technique will be high-stick nymphing. Keep your leader pretty short when fishing with a regular fly fishing rod and reel; you want to keep as much fly line as possible out of the tip to load the rod more easily. A good compromise for the leader is seven to eight feet with a tippet length of two feet.

Most of the time, one nymph will be sufficient, but if you like fishing tandems, the combination of a nymph and a dry fly can be very efficient. You can try the two-nymphs rig only in a very deep pool, where the use of a heavy nymph as point fly will help you reach the bottom quickly. Tie on a smaller fly as the dropper to differentiate the offer.
– *Mauro Mazzo*

DRY FLY FISHING SLOW MEADOW WATERS

Slow meadow waters always appear inviting and easy to fish with trout holding in every bend, but their gentle character belies their fickle nature. Here, the fish will not allow as close an approach as those trout rising in rough water. And myriad currents make drag a constant consideration. Make your cast and watch carefully as the fly approaches a rising fish.

If you see a trout holding, but not rising, try a beetle, ant, or bee straight upstream or slightly across and up. Limit your cast to not more than twenty-five feet. Usually, the fish will come up and take on your first or second offering. Often, it may inspect the fly on the first cast, then move back to its hold. Don't pick your fly off the water too quickly, as many times the fish will come back from its hold and take the fly. If you had pulled your fly off the water, the trout returning to search for it might spot you and spook, or the fish might become suspicious and refuse to look at your next presentation.

When fishing dry caddis patterns on slow meadow water, approach from upstream and cast across and slightly downstream. If you have to approach from downstream, present your fly on a slightly up-and-across angle.

In summer, with so many other insects emerging on smooth flowing waters, many anglers fail to consider midges when they come upon rising trout. There are times, however, when fish will take only impaired or crippled adult midges, even though there may be far more caddis or mayflies present on the water.

Use terrestrial patterns to prospect slow meadow waters. A favorite method on slow meadow waters is to walk the high banks and bluffs of rivers and streams and every few yards creep to the edge of sharp banks and bluffs that overlook the river. You will be amazed at how many fish are in knee-deep water waiting on terrestrials to fall, crawl, or fly into the water. Fish searching for terrestrials will travel considerable distances, so it is always best to have someone watch the fish while the other sneaks up from downstream: it's no use casting to where a fish was instead of where it is.

Mice and frogs inhabit meadow areas along slow meadow waters. Slowly stalk the banks searching for telltale wakes or the backs and dorsal fins of big trout patrolling the shoreline for food. It is best if there is wind or overcast weather to mask your approach. Keep a low profile and search for fish or cast to likely holding water where big trout spend their day; under deep undercut banks, vegetation-covered banks, under overhanging logs or debris, and under log sweepers where big trout escape predators and spend their time waiting for prey to come to them. Remember that a frog or mouse will not swim from one side of the stream to the other when they fall or jump into the water. They always pick the closest place to regain the shore. This requires you to cross back and forth, but the reward can be great.

– Craig Mathews

THE FISHING LIFE

Sam's First Fish
Craig Mathews

Late last summer, I was working with a couple of youngsters learning to fish ten-kara. We were on a small meadow slough in Yellowstone just off the main road

to Old Faithful. I could teach casting techniques to the kids on this tiny pond without concern for wind, brush, or overhanging trees. I knotted on a small grasshopper pattern after cutting the hook point off below the barb for safety. Sam made his first cast ever, a ten footer, against the shoreline, and I told him to twitch the fly then let it sit. He did, and immediately the fly was engulfed in a big swirling rise. I yelled as he yanked back hard on the rod. Since the hook had no point, the fish was gone. Sam asked, "What happened?" All I could offer was, "A big fish hit your fly."

I tied on a fly with a point and the barb mashed down. Sam made another cast, this time a twelve footer. The fly landed with a splat against the shoreline. I told him to twitch it a couple of times, then let it sit still. After a minute, I asked Sam to give the line a short tug. He began to pull the fly, and before it traveled a foot, a fourteen-inch brown slammed it. After a short run and two jumps, Sam towed the fish in, it being no match for 3X tippet. I have a photo of Sam, sporting a toothpaste grin and the fish.

Eleven-year-old Eli Beyer releases a tenkara-caught fish on a backpacking trip in Glacier National Park, Montana. *Jay Beyer*

Spring Creeks

Spring creeks offer the most challenging fly fishing opportunities. They feature constant, clear flows in mixed currents over weed banks and obstructions. To get to know one is to spend much time on its waters. They are often moody and changing, and anglers must adapt to be successful.

Spring creeks are rich with aquatic plants and insects. Idaho. *Steven Wohlwender*

Spring creek trout are usually visible as they actively feed on insect activity like emergences and egg-laying times. Look for fish to be holding in or near weed banks, overhangs, undercuts, downed trees, and brush as well as under bridges. It pays to be patient and spend time observing and sneaking along at a snail's pace learning the creek and its secrets.

WET FLY FISHING SPRING CREEKS

One of the largest spring creeks in the world is the Henry's Fork of the Snake River in Idaho. With its slow-moving water, complex micro-currents created by weed beds, and multiple and complex hatches, it is one of the most challenging streams to fish. Consequently, it attracts some of the best fly fishermen from all over the world.

When there is a hatch happening, it is best to try to match the exact insect, stage, and even gender of the bug that you think they are feeding on. When there are fish rising but there are no visible bugs around, you can often induce the take by fishing a soft-hackle Partridge and Pheasant Tail, which imitates most mayflies.

Cast downstream to the rising fish, except in the summer when floating pieces of grass make it impossible to swing wet flies. In conditions like this, I position myself across from the fish and fish the soft hackle dead drifted like a nymph or emerger. Use only one fly because with a fish on, the other fly will catch on weeds or grass.

The micro-currents that are the bane of the dry fly purist are not a bother with my soft hackle. Also, since I am fishing downstream and the fish never sees my tippet, I don't have to use 6X or 7X tippets, an advantage when landing one of those hefty rainbows.

This is just one example of where the wet fly technique excels on spring creek water.

– *Yvon Chouinard*

NYMPH FISHING SPRING CREEKS

More often than not, it is mandatory to fish upstream and quite far from the fish, in order not to be seen. For this reason, sight fishing at a medium to long distance is the tactic to use. Long leaders are mandatory, together with a very delicate presentation; you want to disturb the water as little as possible.

It is better to use only one nymph, because when sight fishing it is difficult enough to follow the drift of one fly, let alone two. The most effective way to cover this kind of water is to cast a small mayfly imitation up and across to rising fish. I would suggest a Pheasant Tail Nymph tied on a size 16 or 18 hook as universal fly. If you see anything happening close to your fly, like a sudden flash or a shadow covering the fly, strike.

– *Mauro Mazzo*

DRY FLY FISHING SPRING CREEKS

Because spring creeks are so challenging to dry fly fish, successful anglers must be prepared to fish predictable insect activity. Know the weather forecast for the day you are fishing: cool, damp days provide optimal conditions for heavy mayfly hatches.

Blind fishing a spring creek when there are no rising trout only spooks the fish and is seldom productive. There are exceptions, such as during terrestrial periods when grasshoppers, beetles, ants, and butterflies are active; the other is during damselfly and dragonfly periods. This might be the only time anglers see big trout throw caution to the wind and chase natural and artificial flies.

On smaller spring creeks, you seldom need to wade, and if you do, it is only to get into position for a cast. On large spring creeks, you often have to wade to follow fish rising to insects as they move upstream. Always approach rising trout from downstream and present casts to them up and across.

I have had limited success fishing a frog or mouse pattern on spring creeks. But my best luck has been on smaller spring creeks using overhanging vegetation to drop a fly from along deep undercut banks. With just the leader, I merely dap the fly onto the vegetation then pull it off and onto the water. The take is usually immediate and vicious!
– Craig Mathews

THE FISHING LIFE

Fooled by Midges
Craig Mathews

My good friend Terry and I were fishing the Firehole River last spring during epic pale morning dun and caddis emergences. Fish were feeding everywhere along the meadow stretches of the river. We walked to the river and sat on the bank, excited by so many fish we thought were feeding on emerging PMDs or caddis. Instead of taking time to carefully observe the river and determine what the fish were feeding on, we rigged up—Terry with a caddis emerger and I with a PMD mayfly cripple. Several minutes and no fish later, we sloshed to the shore and took out our handy insect nets to sample the flow. There we saw what the river was telling us to do; in the tiny mesh of our insect nets were dozens of midge emergers, many crippled and impaired. We knotted on Zelon midges and each took several rising fish that morning.

Freestone Rivers and Streams

There are few surprises on freestone waters; they are read like an open book, with trout holding where they should in pockets and pools or at

Typical freestone water on a northern section of the Sesia River, Italy. *Mauro Mazzo*

the bottom of riffles and runs. There are always plenty of overhangs, undercuts, sweepers, and rock piles. They include the habitats covered already in the sections on fast mountain and slow meadow waters. And big freestone rivers can be broken down into those fishing situations.

When no insects are bringing fish to the surface on freestone waters, search for trout in riffles, runs, pockets, pools, sweepers, and overhangs. These waters are always cold and some of the last to clear of snowmelt. Insect emergences are later than those on larger waters that warm earlier. Hatches are unpredictable due to late snows or erratic spring weather. All this can make planning to fish them difficult.

WET FLY FISHING FREESTONE RIVERS

The techniques described in the chapter on fishing tenkara with soft hackles apply perfectly to freestone rivers.

If there is no specific hatch on, I would use a size 14 attractor pattern, find some moving water, and work my way downstream. Even if there is a hatch of midges or small mayflies, I often disregard the hatch and stick to an attractor fly. Even during the height of a salmon-fly occurrence, I've been known to continue with a size 14 blue soft hackle . . . and catch my share of rainbows and browns.

– Yvon Chouinard

NYMPH FISHING FREESTONE RIVERS

A freestone river is essentially a bigger mountain stream, and most of the fishing situations are the same. Do not be misled by the dimension of the river; remember that fish are often close to the banks. Don't concentrate only on that pocket in the middle of the river that is impossible to reach; the fish are very often very close to your feet, and if they are not there, it is only because you scared them away.

The Plan River, Alto Adige, Italy.
Mauro Mazzo

Described below are two situations that are unique to freestone rivers. One is a long run of water with a constant depth, and the other is a big pool with a dimension that can often confuse the novice.

A long run of water with a medium current and a depth of two to three feet is prime water for grayling in Europe. Locating the best spots when fish are rising is quite easy, but when there is no surface activity, this water can be difficult to read.

You have to remember that fishing nymphs is an exercise that involves reading the river in three dimensions, not two. So in this kind of water, you will have to look for any submerged rock or any variations of depth that can create a food deposit for the fish. Another indicator to use is the color of the bottom. Dark rocks covered with algae mean a mature bottom, a place where water always flows and where the algae offers perfect habitat for larvae and nymphs. A bottom made of sand or very light and clean rocks means poor habitat or a place that gets dry often—in other words, a place that offers no food.

Once you have located a nice-looking area, the best way to fish it is the classic Czech nymph way—fishing downstream with a short line. Fish the whole width of the river, moving toward the far bank; then walk downstream about ten feet, and come back fishing in the opposite direction.

Another way to cover this water while reducing the chances of scaring the fish—especially when the trout population is predominant—is to fish with a strike indicator. The drawbacks of this technique are discussed in the section on slow meadow water nymphing.

When fishing a big pool with a cascade at the head a good approach is to start from the tail, where usually you will find smaller fish. The water will be quite shallow, so use either two light nymphs or a dry fly and a nymph. My favorite rig is with a dry fly on the dropper, and a nymph as point fly, with about two feet between them.

The dry fly should be highly visible—I am devoted to a Klinkhammer fly, but a parachute fly also works. For the nymph, I suggest the always-effective #14 Pheasant Tail Nymph or Hare's Ear Nymph.

For the deep part of the pool, you can switch the small nymph to the dropper and tie on a heavier nymph as point fly. For this kind of rig, it is advisable to include a piece of fluorescent nylon in your leader to help detect the bite.

Once you are done with the deep part of the pool, you can proceed to fish the head of the pool. This is the most frightening water for a novice as the fast whitewater looks nearly unfishable, but this water often holds the biggest fish. Here you have only one choice: a big and heavy nymph. When fishing a nymph in whitewater, or under a fall, you first have to look for the slower current into which the main current is always broken and fish there.

Do not even try to make a free dead drift; more often than not you will snag your fly. Keep in mind that your fly always has to be kept under control. A way to fish this water is to use a big stonefly nymph and, keeping some tension on the line, let your fly sink till you feel the bottom. Then do a little twitch, to make the fly bounce on the bottom and to avoid snagging.

The best hook to use is a jig, as it works upside down and reduces the chance of snagging the fly on the bottom. The use of big flies, with bodies wrapped with turns of hackles, or made of bulky materials such as dubbed hare's ear, will also reduce the chances of snagging your fly on the bottom.

– *Mauro Mazzo*

DRY FLY FISHING FREESTONE RIVERS

Anglers should always have a few high-floating dry flies for searching this type of water. Bring a basic selection of mayflies, caddis, and stoneflies to imitate those you expect to find. Bring a small selection of terrestrials too. Work upstream and present a short, slack-line cast with a dead drift.

An effective method when approaching risers this closely is called "dapping." Sneak along the bank and keep a low profile while searching for the deepest, outside part of a meander. This is perfect for tenkara as, without casting, you can dap only your fly, tippet, and leader on the water in front of a rising fish.

On this water type, you will find many fish rising in each pool and pocket during mayfly activity. If you are fishing trout rising to a mayfly emergence, position yourself ten to fifteen feet below the rising trout and observe what the fish are rising to, and then present a pin-point-accurate cast. These trout will rise in very narrow feeding lanes, so you must be on target.

On freestone rivers, pick a high-floating, visible caddis pattern that requires little babysitting to keep it floating. An X Caddis is easy to see, floats like a cork, and imitates an impaired or crippled caddis, a stage the trout recognize and take readily.

Stoneflies are usually present on all freestone waters, and you should be prepared to fish stonefly patterns whenever trout are rising to naturals.

But nothing compares to a late-summer day fishing terrestrials or mice and frog patterns on freestone streams. As winter approaches, trout are willing to take most any terrestrial like butterflies, bees, ants and beetles, crickets and grasshoppers, as well as a protein-filled frog or mouse. Fish the edges and overhangs, undercuts, sweepers, and logjams where trout expect to see this list of flies that have fallen into the water. Search all holding water, feeding lanes, seams, and pockets on a short line. With terrestrial flies you should use a drag-free presentation. With mice and frog flies try hopping and swimming the fly back to shore. Don't spend too much time, though, as there will be a beaver dam or spring creek-like section of the freestoner just around the next bend with big trout rising.

– *Craig Mathews*

Kenkara
Craig Mathews

Tenkara is also a useful tool for the seasoned angler. Ken lives along the White
and Norfolk Rivers in Arkansas, where trout are often measured in pounds rather

than inches. On his first visit to our shop in Yellowstone last summer, I showed
him a tenkara rod. He laughed and said something like, "What fish could you
catch with that little stick?" Ken stopped by our fly shop daily, and over the next
several days I caught him discreetly listening to the ongoing discussions on the
merits of tenkara techniques. Finally, one day, acting a bit agitated at our tenkara
tales, Ken said, "OK, I'll bite; just give me one of those dang things, and I'll bet I
break it on a Madison River brown trout today." Two hours later, Ken ran into the
store babbling a story about catching his first nineteen-inch brown trout and several rainbows on his new rod. Today, his email address begins with "Kenkara."

1% For The Planet cofounder Craig
Mathews casts for trout in Idaho.
Tim Davis

Lakes and Ponds

Lakes, ponds, and sloughs will give the fly fisher opportunities to catch larger trout on flies on public water than any other water type.

When searching lakes for fish, look for drop-offs, weed beds, points of land extending into the lake, gravel bars and sandbars, and springs entering, as well as outlets leaving, the lake. Overhanging trees and downed timber provide good food sources and security areas for trout, and sagebrush banks and meadow areas along shorelines can bring grasshoppers, ants, and beetles to the water for fish to feed on. Remember, too, that the largest fish will be near the best security cover.

Trout in lakes are usually on the move as they look for food and the best cover, whereas trout in ponds and sloughs will often be stationary, facing into currents caused by springs or the dammed stream that forms the pond. Always slowly walk the bank, and use waterside cover to locate cruising fish. Be on the water at different times of the day in order to learn when and where the fish move and where their security areas are.

It pays to patiently walk the banks, staying well back from the shoreline. Use the sun to your advantage when stalking the banks for fish. You will be amazed how well trout stand out in sunlight. Nervous water created by fish moving and patrolling for food is a key for anglers to cast well in front of the wakes and strip a streamer or twitch a dry fly on their approach.

Anglers can also fish still waters by wading or from float tubes, boats, and small pontoon boats that are so popular now.

WET FLY FISHING LAKES AND PONDS

Many lakes have leeches, which can be a primary food for lake-dwelling trout. Cast out, let them sink, and fish them with a slow strip with a pause in between strips. The fly needs to have an undulating motion like a swimming leech. Make sure your leech patterns have weight in the front.

All lakes have chironomids (midges), and a soft-hackle midge pattern fished with a twitch is a very effective technique as midges are very active swimmers. At a high-altitude lake in Wyoming, I've watched golden trout come up from twenty feet down to take a size 22 red-body soft hackle on the surface fished in this manner.

If there are caddis, a twitched soft-hackle caddis pattern will be more effective than a dead-drifted floating dry fly.

If there is not much going on insect-wise, try using two flies on light tippets, the point fly being a heavy bead head. Let them sink for

A typical alpine lake, best fished in the early morning or early evening when there is a hatch. Profa Lake, Santa Caterina Valfurva, Italy. *Mauro Mazzo*

as long as you can stand it, and then bring them up to the surface in small strips.

– *Yvon Chouinard*

NYMPH FISHING LAKES AND PONDS

When nymph fishing in lakes, it is imperative to scout around for the places described at the beginning of this section on lakes and ponds. If the wind is blowing, the downwind side of the lake or pond is usual-

Shaun Lawson fights a native lake trout at two in the morning, Great Bear Lake, Northwest Territories, Canada.
Bryan Gregson

ly the best, as most of the food will be taken there by the action of the wind. The use of two or three nymphs will cover more water.

When using a scud imitation, fish it with a nearly still line. Cast your flies as far as possible and let them reach the bottom; then do a little twitch every once in a while to make them more visible to the fish.

When fishing damselfly nymphs or other swimming nymphs, I suggest another approach, which is very useful when using intermediate or sinking lines. When the flies hit the water, count to five (one hundred and one, one hundred and two, etc.)—as a way of knowing what depth you reached—before starting a steady retrieve. If you get a take, you can reproduce that depth on the next cast. If you don't get a take, on the next cast count to seven or eight; repeat, increasing the count until you discover the depth where the fish are. Then carry on fishing at this depth, varying only the retrieve.

– *Mauro Mazzo*

DRY FLY FISHING LAKES AND PONDS

If you want to fish dry flies, be prepared for mayflies, midges, caddis, terrestrials, and damselflies and dragonflies. Be on the water when these insects are active, and they might bring trout to the surface. Few anglers try mice patterns on still waters. Dry mice flies can bring surface action at times, particularly in late evening and into the darkest hours.

On occasion, searching these waters with dry flies can be productive even though no insect activity is bringing trout to the surface. Try terrestrials along brushy banks or areas where overhanging trees bring ants, beetles, bees, or grasshoppers to the water.

If fishing from a float tube or boat, anglers must make sure not to create waves from the boat or float tube by kicking into position. Keep false casting to a minimum, and make sure your presentation is spot on target, as a rising fish will not move from its lane to take a fly.

At all times when fishing a caddis hatch, I use an impaired caddis adult with a trailing shuck like an X or X2 Caddis that floats and skitters well. Cast this dry fly in front of rising fish and strip it into their path with a six- to twelve-inch strip.

On lakes and ponds, midges bring up more trout than any other insect and should be at the top of your list when you see rising trout on still water. Most midge activity occurs during the warmest time of the day when it is calm, which is late afternoon around 6 p.m. Use a crippled or impaired midge adult or an emerging pupa, and get within thirty to thirty-five feet of the rising fish; obviously, you need to use a rod and reel for this type of fishing.

Big trout rising to midges often connect rises every few feet and are those fish that will respond best to proper presentations. They will lock into a feeding rhythm and take adults every few feet. Many times, you will see packs or pairs of fish traveling like wolves and feeding on crippled adult midges caught in their shucks—easy prey. Competition enters in as trout race to the naturals; it is the only time flock shooting works, as you are most certain to get a hit. Present your cast in the path of the rising fish; strike gently to protect your 6X tippet.

One other thing to remember is that after casting it is important to allow enough time to slowly pull on the line to remove slack in the tippet, forcing the fly to come around and face your position. If you fail to do this, the fly will drag even in still water.

Few anglers try mice and frog patterns on still waters. Mice and frog flies can bring surface action at all times, particularly in early morning and late evening hours and into the darkness hours. There is a growing group of hardcore nighttime fishing anglers that can be found arriving on Yellowstone country lakes around midnight to fish. They pitch mice and frog flies along the shoreline and weed beds, next to floating logs or standing dead timber or steep sagebrush-lined banks where mice and frogs frequent to feed under the cover of darkness. Experienced anglers know that big trout feast in the dark of night. The best action is always on nights with no or little moonlight. Fish mice and frog flies on a short line, swimming the patterns as the naturals would when falling or jumping in the water and along the shore, next to weed beds, or near obstructions. Bring a flashlight; you may need it since you might have to throw your tenkara rod when hooking a big nighttime brown trout! This type of fishing can be addicting, I know.
– Craig Mathews

THE FISHING LIFE

Sleeping Trout
Craig Mathews

Last winter we were doing some filming and wanted to get underwater footage of fish feeding on midge pupae before the hatch and fish rising to emerging midges. We arrived, set up, and tried every fly in our boxes before I asked the cameraman to put his tiny underwater camera on a long probe and search nearby rocks and pockets for fish. A minute later, he had me check out his viewfinder, and there was the proof: several trout sleeping next to boulders and logs. We had an early lunch, midges emerged, and the fish came out and fed; we got some nice filming in late that morning.

Another time, my friend Terry and I hiked into a secret lake only to find hundreds of big rainbows in a ball, slowly circling while sleeping along the lake's drop-off. Terry presented a heavily weighted nymph into the ball of trout to wake them up and took a huge rainbow on his first cast. A short while later, mayflies emerged and the fish rose to them; we had a banner day.

Hebgen Lake, Montana. *John Juracek*

The Journey Versus the Destination

Mauro Mazzo

Davide is a good friend who works as a Sesia riverkeeper. For years, he and I had been looking at a very big pool on a nearby river that was nearly impossible to reach. Above and below it were more than 150 feet of sheer rock wall. Because it was so hard to get to, we figured no one had fished it; we thought that a place like that should have plenty of fish and possibly some big ones.

One summer day, we decided it was high time to fish it, and we worked out a plan to reach the pool and gathered the necessary gear. We climbed up to the top of the sidewall, crossed it, rappelled down to the pool, and eventually fished the pool.

Since we thought this would be a day to remember, we decided to take lots of pictures. We started early in the morning, and while Davide climbed the correct side of the rock wall and rappelled down to the pool, I climbed the opposite side of the wall and took pictures of him as he reached the spot. Once he got close to the pool, he stopped and waited for me; the magic moment had to be shared.

So I rappelled down my side of the rock wall, climbed up the right side, and rappelled down again to join Davide. All this took about eight hours, but now we were there, ready to fish the pool that no one had ever fished before.

Davide insisted I had to fish it first. Eager to accept his graciousness, I tied a small nymph on, and as soon as the fly touched the water, I put a little tension on the line, anxious to feel the bite. Nothing. I cast again, waited a little bit more, and nothing. Next, Davide took a turn.

We tried just about every fly and every trick, but we did not get a single touch. We sadly came to the realization that there were no fish at all in the pool. Disappointed, we decided to leave.

We were silent on the way back home, each coming to grips with our failure. But after a while we started talking, and we agreed that although we didn't catch any fish the day was really fun, and we had learned a lesson: it is the journey that is important, not the destination.

Davide rappelling down the Cascata del Tinaccio, on the Artogna River, Italy.
Mauro Mazzo